LIVING WITH APOCALYPSE

Living with Apocalypse

Spiritual Resources for Social Compassion

Edited by TILDEN H. EDWARDS

Harper & Row, Publishers, San Francisco

Cambridge, Hagerstown, New York, Philadelphia

1817   *London, Mexico City, São Paulo, Singapore, Sydney*

Library of Congress Cataloging in Publication Data
Main entry under title:

LIVING WITH APOCALYPSE.

Includes index
1. Spiritual life—Addresses, essays, lectures.
I. Edwards, Tilden.
BV4501.2.L597   1984   261.8   83–48458
ISBN 0–06–062123–0

84 85 86 87 88 10 9 8 7 6 5 4 3 2 1

For those spiritually hungry men and women who come to the Shalem Institute for help with the integration of contemplation and social compassion, that their lives may know and share God's **shalom** *more fully.*

Contents

Acknowledgments

I want to offer special thanks to Monica Maxon for her fine and steady editorial assistance throughout the compilation of this book, and to Gerald May for his editorial comments on selected chapters.

Contributors

TILDEN H. EDWARDS has been the Executive Director of the Shalem Institute, in Washington, D.C., since its founding ten years ago. An Episcopal priest, he is the leader of many groups and programs related to spiritual formation and guidance. His previous books include *Living Simply Through the Day, Spiritual Friend, All God's Children,* and *Sabbath Time.*

CONSTANCE FITZGERALD, O.C.D., is a Carmelite sister and recent prioress of Baltimore Carmel. She is a frequent college and seminary lecturer whose main interest and study aims at reinterpretation of the Carmelite mystics Teresa of Avila and John of the Cross.

JAMES A. FORBES, JR., is Associate Professor of Worship and Homiletics at Union Theological Seminary in New York. His renown as a speaker on the Bible and an interpreter of our times has brought him to speak and consult at major educational and church centers around the world.

JOHN HAUGHEY, S.J., is a research fellow at Woodstock Theological Center, Georgetown University, who concentrates on courses in spirituality for public servants and conversations between members of the military and theologians about the use of nuclear weapons. He is the editor and the author of several books, including *The Conspiracy of God: The Holy Spirit and Us* and *Should Anyone Say Forever? On Making, Keeping and Breaking Commitments.*

ROSEMARY HAUGHTON is a Roman Catholic laywoman and part of a small community at Wellspring House in Gloucester, Massachusetts. Wellspring House is a place of hospitality for people in crisis and the base for Movement for North American Mission, a two-and-a-half-year program for Christians who feel called to serve the poor in North America. Her most recent book is *The Passionate God.*

E. GLENN HINSON is Professor of Religion at Wake Forest University; for many years prior to this he was Professor of Church History at Southern Baptist Theological Seminary in Louisville, Kentucky. He is the author of several books, including *Seekers After Mature Faith* and *A Serious Call to a Contemplative Lifestyle*.

DOLORES R. LECKEY is currently Executive Director of the United States Bishops' Committee on the Laity of the National Conference of Catholic Bishops, and is a member of the Shalem Associate Staff. She is the author of *The Ordinary Way: A Family Spirituality*, reflections on the Rule of Benedict as experienced in contemporary families of various configurations.

JOANNA ROGERS MACY has been a member of the Shalem Associate Staff for many years and has led several Despair and Empowerment workshops for Shalem as well as for other groups. Her newest publication is *Despair and Personal Power in the Nuclear Age*.

GERALD G. MAY is a Board-certified psychiatrist and the Director for Spiritual Guidance at the Shalem Institute. He is the author of five books, most recently, *Care of Mind / Care of Spirit: Psychiatric Dimensions of Spiritual Direction* and *Will and Spirit: A Contemplative Psychology*.

HENRI J. M. NOUWEN is one of the best-known spiritual writers and lecturers in North America. Father Nouwen currently is a member of the faculty of the Harvard Divinity School and was, for many years, on the faculty of the Yale Divinity School. His most recent book, *Gracías*, describes his six-month stay in Bolivia and Peru.

PARKER J. PALMER is a teacher and writer-in-residence at Pendle Hill, a Quaker adult study center and spiritual community in Wallingford, Pennsylvania. He is the author of numerous monographs, essays, and articles about spirituality, education, and social change. His books include *To Know As We Are Known: A Spirituality of Education* and *The Company of Strangers*.

M. BASIL PENNINGTON, O.C.S.O., is a Cistercian monk who lives at Saint Joseph's Abbey in Spencer, Massachusetts. He is a well-known speaker and author of reviews, articles, and books, the most recent of which are *Challenges in Prayer, Monastic Journey to India,* and *Jubilee: A Monk's Journal.*

Introduction:
The Way to a Sound Eye

TILDEN H. EDWARDS, JR.

John and I were taking one of those long aimless walks in the woods that one does on a vacation weekend in the country. He, along with my family, had been invited out by a mutual friend to rest from the tensions of Washington living. Leaving the immediate intensity of our work doesn't necessarily mean escape, though. It can mean perspective.

John is an economist at the World Bank. Along with hundreds of other employees there from countries around the world, he travels a great deal in nations of every variety, assessing their social-economic conditions and efforts at development. As he talked about the growing gap between rich and poor and the ideological and military defensiveness growing apace, he suddenly said with great force, "It is only a real spiritual revolution that can save us," that is, save us from the despair, danger, and impoverishment of becoming permanently armed camps.

Sometime after that weekend I found myself at the World Bank, sitting around a table with a cross-section of twenty-five employees. They had been gathering before work every Friday for almost two years; they came from many countries and religious standpoints. Included among them were long-term veterans of social-political-economic efforts to develop viable social orders around the globe. The one thing they had in common in coming together each week was a sense of disillusionment with the adequacy of their efforts and visions, underlaid by a sense that something vital was missing: an authentic and deep spiritual heart to the quest for a just and humane society. They were hungry for resources that might be brought to bear.

That table we gathered around could be expanded throughout the world to include millions of people who yearn for the spiritual heart that frees the ongoing spiritual revolution toward which God is forever inviting us. Our failure to adequately respond has created ever-clearer warning signals, to the point that the entire world now sits beneath the Damoclean sword of nuclear holocaust.

Living with such an apocalyptic awareness can bring many negative responses, ranging from despair and escape to ever more feverish military buildup on which to depend for security. But a positive response is also possible: The unprecedented power and universal scope of our nuclear predicament can release fresh energies for a deeper understanding of what is wrong with our world and a deeper commitment to what is called for if we are to cooperate with God's vision of *shalom*. *Shalom* is that untranslatable Hebrew word that encompasses the fullness of God's reign in human life and all creation.

Contemplation of what is worthwhile in life from the vantage point of impending death is an old Christian practice. The horror of the nuclear threat provides us with the strange grace of facing into this old practice, whether we want to or not. What do we see when we look back to this life from the precipice of death? I hope we see first what so many people notice when they have been saved from impending death, that is, gratitude. Suddenly we become aware of the precious gift that human life is. We want to affirm it in ourselves and in others. For the moment at least, our best human values are ascendant. What belongs to open compassion and appreciation becomes central. What belongs to closed, fearful self-possession becomes peripheral.

For Christians looking back from the edge of death, God as understood in Jesus Christ can become freshly real and liberating. We are more ready for transformed life that truly serves God's *shalom* in attitude and practice. As we move into life again, we notice with greater pain how separated so many people seem to be from their true and shared life in God—sometimes willfully, sometimes as victims of oppressive social arrangements or ignorance. We see how nuclear threat is only the tip of a vast iceberg of consequences that are entrained by our flawed nature. Finally, we notice the same seeds of separation, the same flaws, still lurking in ourselves, even in the face of our renewed sense of gifted life. We are thus made aware of the battle that continues to rage within and among us for and against God's *shalom*—a battle whose right resolution depends on God's grace and our cooperation.

What spiritual resources can be brought to bear in this battle? How can we be supported over the long haul in our desire for God's fullness within and without?

Looking at life from the vantage point of our death can be such a resource. But this is a secondary one. We must begin farther back, at that bottom level where our most fundamental assumptions of reality are shaped. This is the level Jesus refers to when he says

The eye is the lamp of the body. So, if your eye is sound, your whole body will be full of light; but if your eye is not sound, your whole body will be full of darkness. If then the light in you is darkness, how great the darkness! (Matt. 6:22–23)

This sound eye, in Christian understanding, is shaped slowly by the working of the Holy Spirit in us and by our willingness for this shaping. This brings a lifetime of growing integrity, full of fits and starts, during which all dimensions of our being are attracted toward soundness in Christ: our wills, minds, imaginations, feelings, and bodies. Little by little our whole being is called to conversion from the image into the likeness of God (as the early church fathers like to put it), from Saint Paul's *napioi*, children who must be fed with milk, to *teleoi*, those wise in the Spirit.

Christian tradition has developed a wide range of formational practices over the centuries to encourage this process and to resist delusion and willfulness, which are always just a hair's breadth away. Many of these practices are neglected today for various reasons. Some were used to serve privatistic or elitist views of life; other practices did not adequately understand the gifted, integral relation of mind and body, psyche and spirit, or moral and mystical life. The breakdown of stable community life, exacerbated by the daily bombardments of commercial culture, have further eroded any careful, mutually reinforcing way of life centered in God. An increasing number of people are simply ignorant of available spiritual resources or lack a supporting community in which to sustain them.

Thus we face the enormous threats, confusion, temptations, and possibilities of contemporary life on an intricately interdependent planet with our formational spirituality in disarray. Yet resources are desperately needed for helping us and the world to forge the sound eye we need in order to live with true sustained compassion. Together we need to discern the shapes of *spiritual awareness* and *discipline* that are called for today.

Spiritual awareness for Christians, at its fullest, means seeing life through God's sound eye. We could use other senses to describe this awareness: hearing life through God's ear, touching life through God's strength, feeling life through God's compassion. Jesus revealed our incredible intimacy with the infinite One we call God, so we can dare to speak of being God's senses in the world. Saint Paul called us to live in the mind of Christ so fully that we can say with him, "Not I, but Christ, lives in me." The "I" that no longer lives then is the one that sees itself as an ultimately self-willed, self-centered being. The new "I" is one that lives moment by moment in the awareness that we are an intimate and unique expression of God's joy and compassion, living freely by grace, called to reverberate the joy and compassion, utterly interdependent with Creator and creation.

The test of any spiritual discipline is whether or not it assists this deep awareness for us. Without spiritual discipline we become easier prey to the old "I" that is full of possessiveness, fear, greed, anxiety, violence, indolence, untrustworthiness, willfulness, confusion, and all the other marks of life disconnected from our true being in God.

Spiritual disciplines range from ways of paying attention to grace moment by moment, to ways of reflective understanding, to particular forms of compassion in our called-for daily actions. Some disciplines we keep together as communities of faith; others are called into being uniquely for us at a given time in our lives. Virtually anything constructive *can* be a spiritual discipline if that is our *intention* for it: work, jogging, singing, reading about inspirational people, family life, social action, friendship, as well as the more "direct" disciplines like corporate and personal prayer, fasting, stewardship, scriptural meditation, sacraments, and journal keeping. A discipline thus becomes "spiritual" not so much by its form as by its intent, and authentic intent is tested by the discipline's fruit: Does it lead us to living more constantly in the compassionate and discerning mind of Christ?

In our explosive world situation today, we need to check that our disciplines foster the fruits of *social* as well as individual compassion (though even individual compassion ultimately is social compassion by virtue of the interdependence of all things). We need to ensure that our spiritual attentiveness leads to sensitivity and action that fosters God's just and reconciling peace among the many social configurations of our planet—ethnic, class, and racial groups; nations; deep religious traditions—and between these and our ecological environment (including our own bodies).

What has been called the spiritual life in the past often has had a sad tendency to ignore this wider concern so central to the Church's prophetic tradition. This compartmentalization of the individual spiritual life is, happily, breaking down today. Increasingly, spiritual life is understood as the life of the Spirit in the whole life of the planet, coaxing us toward ever-deeper, liberating communion with one another and witnessing to our shared and gifting Source who empowers our true unity in diversity.

At the same time, it is evident today that those who once tried to collapse the spiritual life into direct action for a just, human community have discovered that God's *shalom* requires more than this. If such action is to be sustained and discerning, it must be rooted in a direct relation to God in prayer, Scripture, and daily attentiveness, not only for the activist, but as part of the goal for the community for whom he or she works. Without a deep spiritual vision, realism about grace and freedom, and sustained discipline, no community can have an adequate foundation for the fullness of life to which we are called. It is hard enough to find our way *with* these. Without them, we lose our orientation to the discerning knowledge of how to be in the world but not of it: alone and together. This knowledge for Christians begins with faith in God for us as revealed in Jesus Christ. It is sustained through time in a rhythm of appreciation and active ministry, both in solitude and with others who form the various dimensions of community to which we are called.[1]

The Shalem Institute for Spiritual Formation in Washington, D.C., was born out of concern for this rhythm.[2] Its special emphasis has been the fostering of deeper contemplative awareness that in turn deepens our discerning faith and compassion. Over the years we have come to realize many particular contributions of contemplative awareness to our quest for God's *shalom*. Perhaps the most important of these is the firsthand awareness of our co-inherence with God and God's creation, a participation in what Jesus declares in many ways: "You are in me, I am in you, I am in the Father."

When we truly realize this co-inherence, we know the communion that is empowered for us through the Incarnation. We realize in this communion our true dignity, wealth, and belonging to all that is of God. This always available 'inside" awareness is the basis for a sound eye that filters light to the rest of the body.

That background of light is brought into the "outside" awareness that can dominate much of our day: our hard sense of self and other, our sense of inner poverty that leads to insecurity and striving, with all the associated temptations of possessiveness, violence, fear, and all the deadly sins that multiply into corrupt and sad societies. The graced light of a sound spiritual eye saves us from overidentifying with this outside mind. It penetrates these constricting, fragmenting, confused, and willful energies and frees them to be seen for what they are and, in God's graced time, to be transformed into energies of connection and bold compassion.

This book grew out of our concern to bring these and related spiritual resources more concretely to bear in the arena of social compassion during this critical historical time. The contributors gathered together for this volume represent many different backgrounds and emphases. But they all share a concern for raising up particular spiritual resources for social compassion in our time. They by no means try to represent a comprehensive or even balanced set of spiritual resources. Rather, they bring to light a highly selective and personal list that is meant to complement the contributions of other writers available today.

Some contributors focus on resources of basic understanding and attitudes. Others focus on particular practical disciplines. Some are members of the Shalem Institute's staff; others have been asked to join us before writing to grapple with their subject. Still others are more distant friends who agreed to make a contribution. All are published authors with long experience behind their writing.

Henri J. M. Nouwen for the past several decades has touched the heart of the spiritual and social struggle of our time for millions of people. He graciously consented to spend a day with our staff, out of which comes "A Conversation with Henri J. M. Nouven." He had recently returned from his first extensive stay in Latin America, which has had significant influence on his understanding of life today. This volume opens with highlights of his provocative and penetrating comments in response to questions we asked him, comments about primary spiritual resources for social compassion, revolution, discipline, contemplation, identity, and suffering.

In "The Spiritual Life: Apocalypse Now," Parker J. Palmer provides us with another broad perspective, based on his extensive experience with the many seekers of spiritual vision from around the world who come to live for a while at Pendle Hill, the Quaker study center near Philadelphia where he has been a central staff member for many years. With the consent of his family, he gave up a promising career as a sociologist in the academic world in order to live a more simple and, for him, authentic life and to explore the possibilities of viable spiritual community for our time. After helping us understand the meaning of apocalypse, Dr. Palmer speaks of particular disciplines of the spiritual life that he finds foundational for compassion: active will, scriptural meditation, silence, and communal life.

James A. Forbes led an electrifying workshop for Shalem on the theme "Spiritual Resources for Social Transformation." As a renowned black Pentecostal preacher and teacher, long concerned for the called-for transformative social consequences of the indwelling Spirit, he provides us with an empowering scriptural foundation for our theme, drawing especially on Jeremiah and Acts. He spells out the biblical process of spiritual formation for participation in the kingdom. His faculty position at the Union Theological Seminary in New York has placed him between many racial, ethnic, denominational, sexual, and political differences that have honed his recent thinking and brought out his great gifts of mediating authentic scriptural understanding across often polarized lines.

M. Basil Pennington continues a focus on scriptural resources by providing us with a simple, classical, daily form of scriptural meditation rooted in monastic tradition: *lectio divina*, with its ingredients of reading (or hearing), meditating, prayer, and contemplation. In a large Shalem gathering of interested people, Father Pennington applied this resource specifically to social compassion. Based on the dialogue then and elsewhere, he has forged this lucid chapter, "*Lectio Divina*: Receiving the Revelation." Through his writings, tapes, talks, and world wide travels, this Cistercian monk has helped to bring the resources of monastic spirituality into the hands of everyday, socially concerned people in the world.

Rosemary Haughton is recognized as one of the most significant Roman Catholic lay theologians of our time. She is British, and for many years she led a pioneering Christian community in southwestern Scotland, a predecessor to the burgeoning lay-led "base Christian communities" around the world today. She now spends most of her time in the United States promoting communities and projects for serious spiritual commitment and social compassion. Her prophetic, theological chapter, "Liberating the Divine Energy," focuses on the fundamental and transforming nature of the divine energy at work in Jesus and us and the liberated imagination we need in order to embody it. She points to the amazing convergences today of modern physics, feminist consciousness, community networks, and Christian mystical and social visionary traditions, and she sees these as vital resources for social compassion. All of these, she finds, express the very material of the universe to be love.

The deepening and broadening awareness today of spiritual resources from various periods of history is opening many rich veins of possibility for us. Four contributors bring to light diverse historical contributions to social compassion in our time.

Constance FitzGerald has for decades sought to understand, teach, and live in the light of the spirituality of her Carmelite community in Baltimore. John of the Cross, a key reformer of Carmelite spirituality in the sixteenth century, along with his close friend Teresa of Avila, is a towering light of Carmelite spirituality, whose radiance, like Teresa's, has reached far beyond the confines of the Carmelite community. Sister Constance orally presented her chapter, "Impasse and Dark Night," to a national group of spiritual writers and leaders, the Ecumenical Institute of Spirituality. It made a powerful impact on those present and struck me as central to the theme of this book. She graciously consented to let us publish it in slightly abridged form. She helps us understand John of the Cross's description of that dimension of spiritual experience called dark night as it applies to our societal experiences of impasse today, experiences for which our culture does not educate us in any meaningful way. With deeper contemplative understanding, she shows us how a dark-night time of human limitation and crisis can become "a learning process for a new vision and harmony," but this requires painful relinquishment of old approaches and a creative re-visioning. She brings to bear many contemporary writers, including many women struggling with impasse, along with her own experience, leaving us with a profound contribution to our way of bearing the social as well as personal impasses experienced by so many people today.

Joanna Rogers Macy brings some very practical resources to our impasse situations (after giving us her understanding of our repression of pain for the world): four specific meditative practices for individuals and groups to release our constricted awareness and action. Her contribution is based on many "despair and empowerment" workshops she has led around the world for people suffering from social despair. She brings to this work not only her Christian background but her extensive knowledge of Buddhism gained in India, in Sri Lanka, and in her doctoral studies in this country. The practices she offers us are adapted from historical Buddhist sources for general use. As she says, "They belong to us all, as part of our planetary heritage." Christian social compassion today needs to include a fresh respect and appreciation for the spiritual resources offered us through other deep traditions that can be appropriated without violence to Christian integrity. The particular classical practices offered us here have been helpful to the numerous Christians struggling with social issues with whom she has worked. They can be adapted and reworded in many ways, depending on one's situation. It seems fitting in a basically Christian volume of resources to remind ourselves that on this shrinking, conflicted planet we need to bring to bear every kind of tested resource that can deepen and sustain our compassion.

John Haughey offers us a practical, daily spiritual practice rooted in Ignatius of Loyola's "Examen of Conscience (or Consciousness)." Ignatius was concerned to develop spiritual practices that would undergird the active worldly compassion to which his Society of Jesus was called in the sixteenth century and ever since. John Haughey stands in this tradition as a contemporary Jesuit whose work and writings reflect his concern for social compassion rooted in a deep personal and corporate spiritual life. In his current position at the Woodstock Center at Georgetown University he has paid a great deal of attention to the social-political situation of the world. In "Hindsight Prayer and Compassion," he focuses on two prayer forms of the Examen that can help us know ourselves before God more fully in order to deal compassionately with the daily situations before us. The first form is a daily examen of our immediate past for purity of intention and for openness to the ongoing call of Christ within our particular vocational situation. The second prayer form is also hindsight prayer, focused on ferreting out the overlooked "love meaning" of our experience.

The final historical contribution comes from the hand of a prominent Southern Baptist church historian, E. Glenn Hinson, who for many years has struggled to strengthen both the spiritual resources and the social vision of that largest of American Protestant denominations. His prophetic article calls for Protestants to incorporate the larger spiritual resources available in Christian tradition and to move more fully into the historical mainstream in ways that do not essentially compromise denominational integrity. Such widening of available resources will in turn widen the possibilities and sustenance for spiritually rooted social concern and action. His focus on Southern Baptists as "a sect becoming catholic" will provide a special challenge and vision for members of that church as well as for other Protestants, and it will be illuminating for those outside these traditions who know little of their recent struggles. Indeed, all churches today, Protestant, Anglican, Orthodox, and Roman Catholic, share in the ongoing struggle between sectarian narrowness and the full vision of the Body of Christ needed in our time. This struggle has many implications for the impoverishment or enriching of spiritual resources for social compassion. Glenn Hinson provides us with, among other things, a schema of current spiritual trends that helps us to look at the strengths and deficiencies of various recent attempts to develop an adequate spirituality.

All of us are (or have been) involved in one way or another with families. This is a confused and struggling arena of life for many people that stands in danger of narcissistically drawing in our energies and isolating family members from the larger concerns of society. Dolores Leckey, out of her personal and educational experience, brings us much fresh clarity and inspiration focused upon the family as sacred shelter: "a place of acceptance, nurture, and growth that empowers family members to participate, according to their unique vocations, in God's ongoing acts of compassion and salvation." She draws out crucial dimensions of family dynamics from selected scriptural passages concerning Jesus and the family, especially aspects of parenting. Dr. Leckey points us to the kind of self-awareness, courage, and confidence of Jesus shown at the age of twelve. She bluntly contrasts what Scripture and other more contemporary writings reveal with certain popular ideals held about the family in our culture today.

Gerald G. May, a colleague on Shalem's core staff who is widely known through his books on psychological and spiritual development, brings his considerable experience as a psychiatrist, and especially as a contemplative Christian, to one of our thorniest problems in social compassion: how to resist destructive and evil behavior out of genuine love rather than out of active or passive aggression. In "Love, Violence, and Apocalypse," he points to those contemplative, wide-awake moments characterized by a temporary suspension of self-consciousness and self-importance as key to this hope. Such moments are an "apocalypse-in-microcosm," when who we really are, including our salvation and destiny, is uncovered. Actions that come out of such awareness will express self-giving compassion in which there is no room for destructiveness. Once we have experienced and continue to recollect the love of those moments, our prayer becomes a way of moving toward this love and of calling upon it as a means of helping ourselves and others. He provides us with some practical ways of discerning whether our proposed action is arising from service of self or personal attachment, or from a heartfelt sense of God's love, and he calls us beyond such discernment to surrender all our intents and agendas to the will of God, along with being honest with God about our resistance to this surrender. Various forms of spiritual guidance are seen as a vital resource in this reflection.

I hope that the experience and practices offered by these authors contribute to your own way to a sound eye, so that together we might more surely move through this apocalyptic time with a discerning trust, compassion, and willingness for God's transforming *shalom*.

NOTES

1. In *Sabbath Time* (New York: Seabury Press, 1982), I spell out this historical Judeo-Christian rhythm of time between Sabbath and Ministry.
2. *Shalem* is a Hebrew adjective cognate to *shalom*, broadly meaning "moving toward wholeness in God."

I. OVERVIEWS

1. A Conversation with Henri J. M. Nouwen

What are you finding to be a central resource for social compassion today?

The new resource for social compassion is in fact a very old resource, too: It is the poor. I went to Peru recently to spend some months living in a poor barrio. I lived in a room put up on the roof of a poor person's house, where I looked out over a sandy desert full of the houses of the poor. Rather than finding myself with lots of time to be helpful, as I had expected, I found that just surviving physically was an accomplishment, as it was for everyone else there.

I first thought that I had to share some of what my privileged environment had bestowed upon me with those who were obviously very poor. This assumption was turned around radically in that impoverished setting. I received more than I could give.

In the parish of a hundred thousand people, seventy percent were younger than twenty. The children came alive for me. When I walked down the road, they were so affectionate, loving, and numerous that I found each finger clutched by a different child wherever I went. They were full of excitement and directness, experiencing life right where they were. They and their parents in countless ways helped to cure the depression and other problems I found I had in my first weeks there. They literally hugged me into health and taught me that life is now, to be shared, and to be thankful for. I found them all reaching out to *me* in concern for my mournfulness. These poorest of the poor knew a certain joy even in the midst of their suffering that was amazing. No one was going to take away their deep awareness of the giftedness of existence in the mystery of God.

How does that lively faith become a revolution?

When it is received! Then this faith is revealed as a gift that can have greater power.

One of the tasks of ministry is to show people their divine gifts. A gift becomes visible in the eyes of the receiver. As ministers, we awaken others to their own qualities by receiving, celebrating, and valuing them, by accepting those gifts and expressing our gratitude. This happens when we interpret something as the grace of God in the other. It becomes revolutionary when the poor can realize their giftedness and know that they have something to give the world. Liberation theology is about claiming that giftedness and setting it free.

One danger I see among nuclear and social protesters, although I support their work totally, is that they can become so dominated by their fear of tomorrow that they miss the gift of the hour. The reality of today does not become a source of liberation for them. They then can become tainted by the very demon they are fighting, and soon they can find themselves turning hateful, aggressive, and violent. You can fight against death only in the strength of life, in God's presence now.

The nuclear threat is not ultimate. We need to believe Jesus' words "I have overcome the world." The world belongs to God. We need to heed the practice Jesus gives us for standing before the Apocalypse in Luke 21:34–36:

But take heed to yourselves lest your hearts be weighed down with dissipation and drunkenness and cares of this life, and that day come upon you suddenly like a snare; for it will come upon all who dwell upon the face of the whole earth. But watch at all times, praying that you may have strength to escape all these things that will take place, and to stand before the Son of man.

Then we can protest as a form of witness to the Living God and not with an anxious soul desperate to change the mind of the President at the last minute. Then our resistance will be an authentic liturgy: the "work of the people" (which is the literal meaning of *liturgy*), making God visible as a God of the living. Protest, then, is an effort to prevent the world from taking away our God-given life. We need to protest all kinds of things that threaten to do this, including the media's great fascination with death. As a *community* of witness, we need to say no to such things on many different levels.

There are many ways of being a peacemaker. We need to experience our own humble task as part of the Body of Christ and encourage others to accept their task. Whatever it is we do, we need to feel *sent* by the community rather than working as isolated individuals. And we need to pray for one another, for our common life and for our common task. Such intercessory prayer is basic to Christian community.

If we are to be peacemakers, it is essential that we take on what I would like to call a mentality of abundance and put away from us the mentality of scarcity. This sense of scarcity makes us desperate, and we turn to competition, hoarding, and a kind of parody of self-preservation. This greed extends not only to material goods but also to knowledge, friendships, and ideas. We worry that everything we possess is threatened. This is especially true in a society that grows more affluent, experiences more opportunities for hoarding and more fears of losing what has been stored, and in the process creates enemies and wars.

We must be willing to give away everything rather than hoard out of a fear that there will not be enough to go around. That is what Jesus shows us in the story of the few loaves and fishes, taken and blessed from an oppressed child, a divine gift that became more than enough for a great crowd. Remember, too, how Jesus told his fishermen disciples to leave everything and follow him, after showing them a great catch of fish that startled them.

This means that we must die to the self focused on scarcity so that we may enter into life trusting in God's abundance. This becomes the basis of real community: We each give what we have to one another. This *fruitful* life is not the same as a *successful* life, though. Fruitfulness is the gift that is given us as a result of our trust in God's presence. Fruitfulness is, in a way, the very opposite of success, of a life focused entirely on *results* and on our attempts to control the future according to our little views and our little survivals.

How do you see the place of spiritual discipline in fostering social compassion?

Every encounter in life involves the spiritual discipline of seeing God in others and making known to others what we have seen. Since our seeing is only partial, we also need other people who will help us to see. Through each encounter, we will come to see more clearly.

Everyone is a different refraction of the same love of God, the same light of the world, coming to us. We need a contemplative discipline for seeing this light. *We* can't see God in the world, only *God* can see God in the world. That is why contemplative life is so essential for the active ministry. If I have discovered God as the center of my being, then the God in me recognizes God in the world. We also then recognize the demons at work in us and the world. The demons are always close, trying to conquer us. The spiritual life requires a constant and vigilant deepening and enlivening of the presence of God in our hearts.

This process includes the real tension of discerning with which eye I see God: my own eye that wants to please and control, or God's eye. Life therefore needs to be lived in an ongoing process of confession and forgiveness. This is the ongoing dynamic of community. The demons lose their power when we confess that we have been in their clutches. The more deeply we confess, the more we will experience the forgiving love of God—and the more deeply we will realize how much more we have to confess. Community life encourages this confession of our demons and our enchantment with them, so that the love of God can reveal itself. Only in confession will the Good News be revealed to us, as the New Testament with its focus on sinners makes clear. One of the great problems with the United States is its refusal to confess its sins. What a great difference it would make, for example, if the President could admit mistakes. The dynamics of social compassion have much to do with both individual and communal forms of confession. It is this that gives us eyes that can see God and the Kingdom in the world.

Can you say something more about the essential place of contemplation, or the mystical life, in this process?

The mystical life is the life by which I grow toward what is real and away from illusion, the life that grows into true relationship. The future of Christianity in the West depends on our ability to live mystically, that is, in touch with that core reality that is the center of events. Without claiming this truth that everything is *in God*, Christianity loses its transforming power and becomes something like "behaving decently," a series of rights and wrongs.

Spiritual discipline involves following the Lord, in the sense of becoming who he says we are, making true what is true, that is, claiming our connected relationship with God and one another and living it out. This is something that is foolish in the eyes of the world, since the world makes us believe that we need all kinds of things that we really don't.

It is out of the privilege of realizing who we really are that we become relevant socially: We want to love more; we admit to evil more clearly in and around us; and we learn to live together in mutual confession and forgiveness. Our power of diagnosis (which literally means "knowing through and through") is deepened, and we can say yes and no to things with more discernment. We become ecumenical in the sense of knowing our connectedness. Indeed, spiritual development is the center of real ecumenism.

This connectedness lies behind the Orthodox Fathers' criterion of holiness: loving one's enemies. As we come to see others' real nature, we realize that God loves our enemies in the same intimate way that we are loved, and that we can forgive them as God forgives them, because it is God forgiving through us.

Ministry in a mystical sense involves an inner freedom that radiates and heals. It thereby means more what we are than what we do. If we give everything to God as Scripture invites us to, then we will find out who our neighbor is and what is needed. We shouldn't worry so much about trying to influence and do good to each other, which, without rootedness in God, can end up being not real ministry but simply a way of dominating one another. Rather, we should concentrate on being faithful and obedient to God, on being "all ears" only to God, listening to God through all things.

What does all this say about our true identity?

Our identity is in the One who loves us. This saves us from our false self, which is anxiously dependent on others' opinions and leads us to sell our souls to the world and to the Evil One who rules the world. The spiritual task is to say that a self defined by others is illusion.

Our true self is in God. As we are told again and again in John's Gospel, we can love others because God first loves us. The spiritual life is coming into touch with that *first* love, which says that we belong to God. As Jesus said, "Just as I don't belong to the world, neither do you"—but you, rather, belong to the Lover who gives you to yourself. We can be a liberating and creative presence in the world only if we don't belong to the world, depend on the world for our real identity. This is the real paradox of ministry: that we can minister to the world only if we don't belong to it.

The depth of our belonging to God is revealed by Jesus. His relation with God through the Holy Spirit is one of total openness. Everything Jesus owns is a gift from the Father. He never claims anything as just his apart from God. He says that we are called to enter the same relationship with the Father as he has, doing all that he does. In sending us the Holy Spirit, he says that we will be led into our full, intimate relationship with God, so that we won't have to be a victim of the world's spirit.

Spiritually we are *in* God, *in* the Lord, *at home* in God. Our true identity is that we are God's children. From that perspective, we perceive the world, that is, from God's perspective. We are called to see the world as God sees it; that is what theology is all about. Therefore, we are continually diagnosing the illusory quality of anything outside this perspective.

What other spiritual resources help us with this perspective?

Following the liturgical year, with its seasons and days of commemoration, can help us understand this because it shows us

God taking place in history as a continual event. It helps us answer the basic ongoing question, What's happening? What's happening is that God is in our midst, is born among us, is suffering in us, rising up with hope, sending the Spirit. This contrasts with the bored, empty answers we usually get when we ask each other that question on the street: "What's up?" and we hear, "Oh, nothing much."

Resources like Scripture, the Church, the Eucharist, individual spiritual guidance, and our own hearts also can tell us that what's happening belongs to God. And this includes ourselves. They can help us connect our own story to God's story. They can help us to see that we are an ongoing revelation of God and to claim our own suffering and joy as part of God's. Our great temptation is to *disconnect* our story from God's story. Compassion comes from *making* these connections.

How can we deal with the church community that does not respond to calls for compassion and a real awareness of God in life?

The value of the spiritual life is not in the *numbers* who live it. God loves everyone, but some are elected as a creative minority to witness with a burning love for God. Jesus never predicts that everyone will love one another. He said there will be persecution, but don't worry—you will know what to say when the time comes. Even death can't take life away from you.

What do you say to people who ask why God lets us suffer?

I don't say anything. The question really means there is deep personal suffering. Allow the question to be there. By your own solidarity with the question, you reveal the solidarity of God with that suffering. God loves us so much that he does not simply take our suffering away: He suffers with us. If we understand God's solidarity, the One who did not cling to power but gave it up, who did not cling to the ability to solve everyone's problems—that is to have the mind of Jesus Christ. Be present to each other and experience in the depths the gift of life! Christ didn't fall into solutions or solving problems—that's the temptation of the desert. That's our temptation—to solve people's problems, to cure, not care. To care means being where the suffering is. It's a way of living together so the mystery of life is revealed.

There is joyful solidarity with humanity. You are part of the human struggle. I am so human I can struggle with others. That is the strength revealed by the people in Latin America—to be connected with humanity and thus to be connected with Christ. Be part of that salvific event! You can take it all on! Jesus said, "Shoulder my yoke . . . my yoke is easy and my burden light." That's what the mystical life is all about.

2. The Spiritual Life: Apocalypse Now

PARKER J. PALMER

Apocalypse is a word to stop conversations, not start them— hardly a promising word with which to begin a chapter or a book. *Apocalypse* suggests the annihilation of life as we know it, live it, and love it, a moment of blinding brilliance fading into eternal darkness when all we are and have and do will be blown away in fury and in fire. For a brief time in our history, between the rise of rational secularism and 1945, we could dismiss apocalyptic thinking as a fanciful phase of spiritual speculation. But today, when nations possess the weaponry to bring human history to an end, *apocalypse* is a political term, a very *un*fanciful reality in our daily lives. It is a word before which a writer—at least this writer—quails. Before it, all my other words seem to turn to dust.

But a writer owes a duty to language, the honor of taking it seriously. Our words have hidden histories and meanings buried under centuries of conventional use. We can unearth the buried wisdom of our words by going to their roots and touching their original meanings; our words often say more than we know and know more than we say. So it is with the word *apocalypse* whose root is a Greek term that means "to uncover, to reveal."

The destruction of life as we know it is not the primary meaning of *apocalypse*. Instead, it means revelation—the uncovering of a beauty and sacredness in life that have been obscured by our ways of knowing, living, and loving. Our apocalypse is here because we have lived in illusions, especially the illusion of human power. It is a time of disillusionment, of the failure of our fantasies in the face of God's own truth. So apocalypse *may* not be an end but a new beginning, a time when we are invited into the power of the spiritual life. Whether it *will* be a new beginning depends on our understanding of spiritual truth and our capacity to follow its call.

In this chapter I want to show how the nuclear apocalypse is uncovering, peeling back, the layers of illusion that have obscured the ground of our life. First, I look at the layer of factual rationality on which the modern world has built, only to learn that it has built on sand. Second, I look at the layer of emotion and feeling in which some of us are now finding new power and guidance for life—but in which I suspect we will discover as much self-deception as we have in rationality. Third, I explore the spiritual ground that lies beneath our despairing facts and ambiguous feelings, asking what that ground is and how we can sink our roots more deeply into it. For it is only in the life of the Spirit that apocalypse can turn from the omega of end time to the alpha of healing and hope.

FACTS, FEELINGS, AND FAITH

Jonathan Schell, in his searching analysis of *The Fate of the Earth,* has described the role of the fact-obsessed mind in the creation of our nuclear apocalypse:

The fundamental origin of the peril of human extinction by nuclear arms lies not in any particular social or political circumstances of our time but in the attainment by mankind as a whole, after millennia of scientific progress, of a certain level of knowledge of the physical universe. . . .To return to safety through technical measures alone, we would have to disarm matter itself, converting it back into its relatively safe, inert, nonexplosive nineteenth-century Newtonian state—something that not even the physics of our time can teach us how to do. . . .

It is fundamental to the shape and character of the nuclear predicament that its origins lie in scientific knowledge rather than in social circumstances. . . .

Scientific progress (which can and certainly will occur) offers little more hope than scientific regression (which probably cannot occur) of giving us relief from the nuclear peril. . . . In the centuries of the modern scientific revolution, scientific knowledge has steadily increased the destructiveness of warfare, for it is in the very nature of knowledge, apparently, to increase our might rather than to diminish it.[1]

Schell's retelling of modern history is, of course, a tale well known in prehistorical myth, a fact recognized by Robert Oppenheimer who, after the bombings of Hiroshima and Nagasaki, said, "The physicists have known sin." It is the tale of Adam and Eve who hungered for ultimate knowledge of good and evil and were driven from Paradise by God. Their sin (and ours) was not the desire for knowledge, and its expiation is not to be found in ignorance. Their sin (and ours) was the *kind* of knowledge they sought—a knowledge that distrusted God, excluded God, denied God; a knowledge that would make gods of the knowers themselves. Adam and Eve were driven from the Garden not by a God who wishes to keep us in ignorance, but by a God who has no peer. That myth (and our own history) tells us the knowledge that glorifies not God but the knower will drive us into the desert, into apocalyptic times.

We are "fact" seekers, and that word too has instructive origins. It comes from the Latin *facere*, "to make," a meaning seen most clearly in our words "manufacture" and "artifact." Facts are things manufactured by human hands, and with our facts we try to make ourselves a world. It is no accident that our obsession with facts has grown as our faith has declined—the faith, I mean, that a world has been made for us with us as creatures in it. We no longer see ourselves as recipients of a world-as-gift; we no longer regard knowing as a way of receiving and celebrating that gift. Now we alone are the creators, building a world by the sweat of what lies behind our brows, a task we pursue with pride at our power and success. But now we proceed with trembling, for we have begun to sense the precariousness of this mind-made world. When the world is what we make it, we can unmake it at any time—and that is exactly what our sinful knowledge now threatens to do.[2]

In these apocalyptic times, many people schooled in the cool facticity of science have had a revelation. We have discovered that facts are not enough to guide us and sustain us; we have uncovered the life of feelings that lies beneath the life of facts. Beneath the pride and power of intellect with its self-confident certainties, we have uncovered feelings of powerlessness, abandonment, and terror that science can neither comprehend nor assuage.

We are learning that the road to personal and social health requires that we acknowledge and express such feelings, drawing them up from hiddenness and repression and sharing them with one another. Failing to do so, we have no capacity for compassion, a concept that means literally "to feel with" another, to suffer another's suffering, to enjoy another's joys. If we cannot feel our own feelings, we surely cannot feel another's. And lacking such compassion, numbed and isolated, we can create no counterforce to the apocalyptic powers.

This recovery of feelings has been a movement toward wholeness and health. It has had its excess, of course—a tendency to deny the mind altogether and rely on emotions alone. But at its best, this movement toward feelings has been a search for integration, a way of allying the head with the heart. Yet even as we identify, explore, and share our feelings, we must ask whether those feelings are any more reliable than facts as sources of nurture and guidance in apocalyptic times. Facts and feelings, however much they may differ, have this much in common: They are generated by the self, a self that seems to have an endless repertoire of self-deluding and self-defeating ways. We have learned that the world we build with our facts is ultimately precarious. Is a world built upon feelings any more sound?

I know a great many people who have been "working with their feelings" in recent years, and although that work has been important to them, I (and some of them also) suspect that feelings that are not followed into a deeper reality take us to dead-ends. It is vital to express and explore our feelings in all of our relationships—in marriage, in community, with the larger world, with God. But when the only response to feelings is more feelings, we tend to get caught in a magic circle of emotions. We find ourselves expressing the same feelings again and again, recycling them in a process that creates its own despair. While we cry out, the principalities and powers of death (which are in us as well as in our world) remain unmoved, for they are incapable of compassion. If the flood of dark feelings has no outlet into a larger ocean of light, we run the risk of drowning in them.

I have noticed another problem in this work with feelings. Sometimes, when we enter into the dark places of our emotional lives, we experience in the midst of turbulence moments when we seem to live in a peace that is beyond our emotions. I have talked with troubled people who find respite, even transcendence, in simple friendship, simple work, simple silence. But when feelings are their ultimate guide to reality, they tend to deny those moments of peace. They accuse themselves of merely suppressing their feelings at those moments, of allowing themselves to be distracted from the painful realities of an apocalyptic world. Lacking a way of understanding these experiences within the framework of either facts or feelings, they discredit and invalidate "the peace which passes all understanding."

I believe that such moments of peace are clues to the spiritual life that lies beneath the life of facts and the life of feelings. If we are to multiply and magnify those moments in ourselves and in the world—and that is the vocation of peacemakers—we must come to understand the reality of the spiritual life itself. If we are to turn our apocalypse from an end into a new beginning, we must learn to recognize the movement of the Spirit that is tracked neither by feelings nor by facts but by faith alone.

THE LIFE OF THE SPIRIT

What is the spiritual life? Volumes have been written on the subject. But with seventeen simple words, Paul offers a summary of spiritual experience that I find unsurpassed: "I am crucified with Christ, but I live; yet not I live but Christ lives in me" (Gal. 2:20). The spiritual life, Paul tells us, has three basic movements, which relate to facts and feelings, but move in us more deeply than our minds and emotions can know.

First, "I am crucified with Christ. . . ." Here the spiritual life begins, with immersion in darkness and pain, with the experience of crucifixion. How different this is from the popular notion that spirituality begins on a mountain top, in "peak experiences." We yearn for such experiences, and from time to time they come our way. But they do not stay. What stays is the sense of apocalypse, the deepening struggle with losses and betrayals and deaths, little and large. Of course our lives are made of joy as well as sorrow, and of much more in between. But time and again life takes us to the valley of the shadow, and we must learn to find light there.

The spiritual life begins with crucifixion because at those moments we lose our illusions. We realize then that we are neither wise nor wily enough to defeat the powers of darkness. We learn then of our own insufficiency. We turn then to the sufficiency of the Spirit.

But Paul says more than "I am crucified." He says, "I am crucified *with* Christ. . . ." Paul knows that the Spirit we need to turn to has already turned to us. This is the deep meaning of God's compassion for us, and the deep source of our compassion for one another: God suffers with us. The Spirit is no classic hero, riding in to snatch us from distress. The Spirit does an even braver thing by standing with us, sharing our condition, even in the darkest and most demonic of our midnight hours. As we become aware of this Presence in the midst of our crucifixions, the spiritual life begins. As we become able to stand with each other in the Spirit, the life of compassion begins.

Second, ". . . but I live. . . ." We can almost hear the surprise and elation as Paul gives voice to this second stage of the spiritual life: Though I have sojourned in the land of the dead, I live! Death is not victorious but is conquered by life in the Spirit! How startling it is, in the depths of long bouts with depression and despair, to discover that there is within us an inextinguishable spark that persists, insists on living. Sadly, not everyone can see that spark. But when we have seen it we want to fan it into larger and brighter flames. Today we are surrounded by techniques for fanning the fire, methods of expressing and receiving the warmth of feeling that burn beneath our cold world of facts.

There is healing in these efforts to revive the emotional life in our crucified sense of self—I know that from personal experience. Though the spiritual goal is ultimately to lose ourselves so we can find ourselves, we must first have a self to lose. But in these efforts there is also spiritual danger. If we do not move beyond the discovery that "I live!" we quickly fall back into illusions about our own sufficiency, forgetting our need for the sufficiency of the Spirit. By strengthening our feeling-self and celebrating the survivor-self, we can become isolated, not only from others who need our compassion, but from our own need to receive God's compassion for us. The winds of the cold world blow hard, and they easily blow out the flame of the human self. If we confuse that inextinguishable spark with our own ego-self and fail to see it as a glimpse of God's eternal light, we are only setting the stage for a continuing cycle of crucifixions. There is a difference between psychological coping and living the spiritual life—and the difference lies in how we answer this question: Who is it who lives within us in the dark night of our souls?

Third, ". . . yet not I live, but Christ lives in me." Here is the ultimate surprise in Paul's summary of the spiritual journey. The life he feels within him is not a biological will-to-live, not his own resurgent ego, not the vibrancy of resurrected feelings. It is another life within him, the life of God's indwelling Spirit. This Spirit not only suffers with us in our crucifixions, this Spirit overcomes the powers of death; it lives in and through us even—and especially—when the human self succumbs.

What is the spiritual life? It is not "our" life, but the life of the Spirit within us. It is not a life we live, it is a life that wants to live us. It is not a life we lead, it is a life that wants to lead us. It is not a life we create with our facts or with our feelings. It is life as gift that we need only open ourselves to receive.

In the spiritual life, we learn that neither facts nor feelings define reality. The facts in life may be ominous, but there is a Spirit life full of hope and grace. My feelings may not be loving: I may be filled with greed or anger or despair. But beyond my life of feelings there is still a life of love, a life for which my feelings are no measure.

With Paul's discovery that "Christ lives in me" the contortions and confusions of spiritual experience suddenly make sense. Crucifixion is necessary, inevitable, for only by dying to our false selves can the Spirit-self emerge. We are led to rejoice "I live!" not to celebrate our ego strength but to learn where the power for life comes from. In that power, our life is no longer our own. Now it is a life for God and a life for others. In that power we not only survive but witness and serve—able to take risks, to dare ventures, to offer ourselves to the works of mercy far beyond our own capacity to give.

IMITATIVE ACTION

How must we live in apocalyptic times to uncover—to reveal—to ourselves and others the power of the spiritual life? What are the disciplines by which we can see and respond to the life being lived in us in a world that seems dominated by death? What are the sources of compassion in apocalyptic times?

Earlier in this chapter, I referred to "the works of mercy" as one of the fruits of the spiritual life. It is no mere coincidence that these works are described in one of the most powerful apocalyptic passages in the Gospels—for apocalypse reveals what our spiritual work must be:

When the Son of man comes in his glory, and all the angels with him, then he will sit on his glorious throne. Before him will be gathered all the nations, and he will separate them one from another as a shepherd separates the sheep from the goats, and he will place the sheep at his right hand, but the goats at the left. Then the King will say to those at his right hand, "Come, O blessed of my Father, inherit the kingdom prepared for you from the foundation of the world; for I was hungry and you gave me food, I was thirsty and you gave me drink, I was a stranger and you welcomed me, I was naked and you clothed me, I was sick and you visited me, I was in prison and you came to me. . . . Truly, I say to you, as you did it to one of the least of these my brethren, you did it to me." Then he will say to those at his left hand, "Depart from me, you cursed, into the eternal fire prepared for the devil and his angels; for I was hungry and you gave me no food, I was thirsty and you gave me no drink, I was a stranger and you did not welcome me, naked and you did not clothe me, sick and in prison and you did not visit me. . . . Truly, I say to you, as you did it not to one of the least of these, you did it not to me." (Matt. 25:31 ff.)

These merciful works are among the fruits of the spiritual life, but they are at its roots as well. It is not simply that we discover the life of the Spirit within us and then go out to do works of mercy. It is also the case that when we go out to do compassionate work we discover the Spirit life in ourselves and others. We may not "know" or "feel" mercy in ourselves or in the world, but if we can act mercifully we will discover the mercy that is there.

This is the first spiritual discipline I want to mention—the discipline of action—simply because it marked a major turning point in my own spiritual journey. Ten years ago, after years of thinking and prayer about the possibility of living in a spiritual community, my wife and I decided to visit some communities where people were doing just that. On a visit to Koinonia Partners in Georgia, someone said words of revelation to us: "You don't think your way into a new kind of living. You live your way into a new kind of thinking." His words rang so true that we simply left what we were doing and moved into the Quaker community at Pendle Hill, where we have been ever since. That action made all the difference.

Of course, my friend overstated the case. Our thinking and praying had prepared the soil to receive his words. But his counsel is a caution against the dangers of our linear, deductive approach to life: First think and pray, establish some principles and premises, then act upon them. That may be the way the life of facts operates, but not the life of the Spirit. The linear approach almost always becomes an infinite regress, always receding into finer and finer analyses while postponing the action that might reveal life anew to us.

Action is revelatory. What we know about life is a function of where we stand in it, and by acting we take up a new standpoint. The man or woman who stands in society as an unquestioning, law-abiding taxpayer sees one reality. But the person who questions the proportion of our taxes that goes to making war, who turns that question into even the smallest action (like paying the tax under protest), begins to see things anew. Such a person recalls the lesson of history that society's most "sensible" demands are sometimes morally wrong. Such a person discovers an inner capacity for moral resistance that he or she was not aware of before.

The discipline of action can also be called the discipline of will. Beneath our capacity to perceive facts and feel feelings we have the capacity to will our lives into places where new facts and feelings can emerge. Our analytic minds have a way of always calling for one more fact, one more reason, before they allow us to act. Our emotions, as powerful as they can be in goading us to action, have a way of chasing themselves around in a deepening cycle of despair. Will is the agency by which we can break the iron cage of facts and feelings. But what shall we will?

For Christians, the answer can be found in the ancient concept of *imitatio*, the imitation of Christ. Scripture tells the story of a life of compassionate action; we can will to imitate that life even when our facts and feelings lag behind. Such imitation is much like the "patterning" therapy that has been used successfully with brain-damaged children. Parents and friends spend endless hours moving the child's arms and legs in normal, healthy patterns; as they do so, healthy connections within the brain are renewed. By imitating the movements of a healthy child, we help create genuine health within the damaged one.

I realize that the concept of *imitatio* sounds dishonest in our psychologically sophisticated culture; we think it is fraudulent to act out something we do not feel. But patterning therapy suggests that "going through the motions" is not as bad as the idiom suggests. Even on the basic level of physiology, we apparently do "act our way into a new kind of thinking!" Our feelings are inadequate guides to the life of the Spirit. As we pattern our will and actions after the life of Christ, we are allowing the body's movements to form a new Spirit within.

To imitate the life of Christ we must first know that life. So here is the second spiritual discipline I want to explore—the discipline of studying the Christ-life as portrayed in Scripture. We live in a different time than Jesus did, and we are radically different persons. But his life is portrayed for us in a story whose patterns and forms transcend space and time and personal differences. The "information" we have about his life is exactly that: in-formation that can inwardly form us as we study and respond to the outward patterns of his life.

Our fact-seeking minds have a way of diminishing the inward meaning of information. The story is told of Daniel Webster and the Devil walking down the road one day and coming across a sack labeled "Truth." As the Devil walked on by, Webster said with surprise, "I thought you would pick up that sack and destroy it." "No need," said the Devil. "Some scholar will come along and organize it and accomplish the same result." Our minds, with their tendency to make logical sense of the information we receive, to form it in their own image of validity, diminish the power of information to inwardly re-form us.

So we must learn to study Scripture in a different way, the way called *lectio divina* in the monastic tradition. This is "sacred reading," a slow, prayerful, interactive way of not only reading Scripture but letting it read us. In *lectio divina* we abandon our speed-reading strategy of mastering the facts in favor of living with a page, a passage, or a line for hours or days at a time so that truth has a chance to invade and master us. (Basil Pennington gives us his own understanding of this discipline elsewhere in this volume.)

The search for truth in Scripture is, as the root of "truth" suggests, a search for troth, for a living relationship with the life portrayed in those texts. The way *lectio divina* can help us enter into troth with Jesus Christ has been described by the monk Thomas Keating:

> Christianity is not centered around a moral teaching, but around a person. . . . The scripture is the normal way of introducing us gradually to the knowledge and love of this person. This process involves the kind of dynamic that happens in making friends with anyone. You have to spend time together, talk together, listen to each other, and get to know each other. At first you feel a little awkward and strange in one another's company, but as you get better acquainted, and especially as you feel yourself going out to the goodness you perceive in each other, the amount of time spent in conversation begins to diminish. You are at ease to rest in one another's presence with just a happy sense of well-being.
>
> The process that I have spoken of in terms of human friendship is the way *lectio divina* works too. In a sense, it is a methodless way of meditation. It does not depend on some particular technique, but on the natural evolution of friendship. . . . It is a personal exchange.[3]

To engage in this personal exchange, this friendship, is the highest meaning of "imitating" Jesus Christ. We are not to follow the patterns of his life mechanically or slavishly; that would only make us puppet-forms of our true selves. Instead, we are to follow Jesus in the way we would follow a friend, always alert for the resonances and dissonances of two independent people trying to live in a bond of truth, of mutual fidelity. As we do so, we discover our own lives being inwardly re-formed by a living relationship with one who loves us and wants to set us free.

Recently, meditating on Luke's Gospel, I have become aware of some of the patterns of the Christ-life in history that help me sense the shape of the Christ-life in myself. Let me reflect briefly on two of them—the period of expectant waiting that precedes the birth of Christ, and the movement from hiddenness to public ministry that occurs in the middle of the story.

Much of my spiritual life is spent waiting expectantly for the Spirit to make itself known. But my waiting, unlike the waiting of Mary, often makes me weary and discouraged as nothing seems to come. I realize now that Mary's waiting is very different from mine. Whereas I wait for something "out there" to come my way—a friend, a job, an event, or peace itself—Mary waited for something "in here," for a vitality whose seed was already within her. This transformed her waiting; it was not anxious, as mine is, but expectant, full of the knowledge that God had done a work in her that she had only to bring to term. This insight has begun to transform my waiting. I realize now that I am waiting not for God's work in me, which has already happened, but for my own response—and that realization opens up possibilities for action every moment of the day.

As I study the movement of Jesus' life from hiddenness to public ministry, I become aware how difficult these two phases of my life are for me. Apocalyptic times demand public faith, public witness, public action—and my own work seems so hidden and insignificant in the face of these demands. But when I do "go public," the stresses and strains are so intense that I long to return to the hidden life. Reading the Christ story in Luke, I become more deeply in-formed in relation to this struggle. We know little about the hidden first thirty years of Jesus' life, except that he "advanced in wisdom and in stature" with God and with people. But with that, we know a great deal; we are reminded that our own times of hiddenness can be a deepening in the life of the Spirit. Then we learn that as Jesus moved into the public ministry, he did not leave hiddenness behind; he frequently left the crowd for times of solitude and prayer, and he often spoke to the crowd in the hiddenness of parables. Knowing this reminds me that withstanding the rigors of public ministry requires the hiddenness of the inward life, that the two movements belong together, like breathing in and breathing out.

COMMUNITY AND SILENCE

The final form of the Christ story in Luke-Acts is the flowering of the Church, of spiritual community. Community, like compassionate action, is both a fruit and a root of the spiritual life. So I will discuss community as the third discipline of spiritual discovery. It is the overarching discipline in which both our action and our prayerful reading must be couched.

Our fact-obsessed culture tells us that data and logic are our guides to the nature of reality. Our growing culture of feelings tells us that emotion and instinct are more reliable guides to what reality is like. But spiritual reality, ultimate reality, is finally defined neither by facts nor by feelings but by faithful relationships, by community. We are in community with God, and through God with each other and the whole created world, in a community of mutuality and accountability, of the truth that is troth. If we are to discover the communal nature of reality we must live and learn, act and pray, in communities that are microcosms of the cosmos that God gives us.

We do not find community by seeking it out as an end in itself. Instead, community finds *us* as we pray about and act upon the concerns that are closest to our hearts. This is the lesson of the liberation communities that have grown strong in our apocalyptic times—the black movement, the women's movement, the peace movement itself. These communities came into being as isolated individuals saw deep into the conditions that enslaved their lives, acted on what they saw, and found community with others who were fighting the same fight. Prayer and action not only reveal the Spirit of community that lives within us, prayer and action allow that Spirit to form us into the image of the community that we seek.

But as we wait for community to find us, what are we waiting for? Too often our hopes are shaped by false images of community, images of instant peace and harmony, healing and light. When we first discover each other, in the first flush of communal romance, we think we have found just that. But soon the hard realities of relationship begin to be felt. We feel hurt as well as healing, conflict as well as harmony, darkness as well as light. These experiences do not fit our romantic image, so we abandon each other, thinking, This cannot be the community I seek. We return to our isolation, perhaps to wait once more for true community to come, but now our expectancy is diminished by the skepticism and cynicism that come in the wake of failed fantasies.

Perhaps we can find guidance in some biblical images of community. Two of them are images of perfect harmony, perfect peace. One is the Garden of Eden, where man and woman walked naked and unashamed, vulnerable to each other and—for a while—without fear. The other is the eschatological vision of the Kingdom of God, where every tear shall be wiped away. But both of these perfect images are out of history, out of the arena in which we must live our lives: The Garden of Eden comes before history begins, and the Kingdom of God arrives after history ends. If these are the only images that inform our waiting for community, we will wait a long, long time.

But the Scriptures also contain an image of community in the here and now. It is the image of the Last Supper, where Jesus gathers the disciples around the table to break bread and share the cup. What happens in this tale of community here and now? The bread and drink of life are shared, yes. But Jesus says that someone at the table will betray him, and the disciples wonder who this may be. They do not spend much time wondering, they soon fall into an argument about who is the greatest among them. Probably, as one wag has suggested, they even quarreled about who would pay the bill! It is like every community I have ever been part of—people trust and people betray, people share and people fight for power. If I want community, I cannot flee from these disillusionments and pains, for they are part and parcel of the community I seek. Instead, I must learn to do what Jesus did—to stay at the table, to continue to share the bread and wine of life.

The images of the Garden and the Kingdom are not irrelevant here; in fact, we can assume that Jesus carried these images with him. The Garden is an image of memory, the memory of how we were originally formed in community with each other and with God. The Kingdom is an image of hope, the hope that comes from knowing a God who has already broken into our history with reconciling power. Memory and hope are vital disciplines if we are to stay at the table.

I have lived in a spiritual community for ten years now. We spend a great deal of time wrestling with facts—the facts of the world we want to minister to, the facts we must face to stay solvent and sound. We also spend much time struggling with our feelings, with the frictions that arise daily when seventy people live so closely. But I do not think we could stay at the table without our daily discipline of silent worship, that morning gathering when we allow ourselves to sink beneath our facts and feelings into the presence of the Spirit who lives within and among us. So often we feel more community in that silence than at any other time of day—not because we are suppressing difficult facts and feelings, but because in the Spirit we are transcending them. The daily discipline of silent worship allows us to sense the reality of a spiritual life that lies beyond our minds and our emotions.

So let me name silence, personal and corporate silence, as a fourth discipline of the spiritual life in apocalyptic times. Silence is apocalyptic in itself, at least for those of us who have built our lives on facts and feelings. For in the silence all these constructs of our minds and hearts are devastated, blown away. In the silence we experience the uncovering, the revealing, of the Spirit life that wants to live in us and through us.

I still recall my own silent apocalypse some ten years ago. At first, I found this way of worship restful and rewarding. But before long, dark feelings emerged. I found myself upset, even angry; having been raised in a liturgical tradition, I began to feel that silence was a fraud. No word was read or preached, no hymns of praise were sung. What kind of worship was this, after all?

A few friends recognized my anger—which took no intuition, I had become quite vocal about it!—and asked me to reflect more deeply on its sources. With their help, I understood the problem. I had come to the silence with a headful of religious ideas and beliefs. In the silence, they all fell away, structures without foundations. In the silence I was forced to confront the ambiguities of my own religious experience, and I grew angry about what I found there, about the discrepancies between my inherited faith and my own faithless life.

As we move into the silence toward the reality of the Spirit, we must first go through the experience of God's absence. This is a moment of apocalypse, as our theories crumble and a vast emptiness opens before us, a vision of our inner world as a trackless desert in which the living water is nowhere to be seen. But this is also an apocalypse of potential revelation or uncovering, which may happen in the way described by Louis Dupré:

If fully lived through, the emptiness of one's own heart may turn into a powerful cry for the One who is not there. . . . Here, the very godlessness of the world is invested with religious meaning, and another dimension opens up in this negative encounter with a world that has lost its divine presence. Thus the believer learns that God is entirely beyond his reach, that He is not an object but an absolute demand, that to accept Him is not to accept a "given," but a Giving.[4]

Through the discipline of silence, we learn that before we can give compassion to others, we must accept God's Giving. Our own inner apocalypse can turn us toward a Spirit that, in the words of James Nayler, "delights to do no evil, nor to avenge any wrong, but delights to endure all things, in hope to enjoy its own in the end."[5] The apocalyptic end time, inwardly and outwardly, is a time for uncovering the possibilities of life and love in the Spirit.

PRAY TO LIVE

I have said little in this chapter about the concrete and specific acts of compassion we must undertake to turn the nuclear apocalypse from an end time into a new beginning. The possibilities for such acts are endless and imperative; each of us must discover them in his or her own situation. I have tried, instead, to speak about the spiritual life that is the foundation for compassion, without which our acts will be weak and short-lived. We discover the reality of this life that lives in us through the disciplines of active will, *lectio divina*, and silence, all set within the discipline of communal life together. Pray and live that this apocalypse may be a time not of endings but of new beginnings in the Spirit who calls us beyond death into life.

NOTES

1. Jonathan Schell, *The Fate of the Earth* (New York: Knopf, 1982), pp. 100, 106.
2. For a fuller treatment of this theme, see Parker J. Palmer, *To Know As We Are Known: A Spirituality of Education* (San Francisco: Harper & Row, 1983).
3. Thomas Keating, *The Heart of the World* (New York: Crossroad, 1981), pp. 45–46.
4. Louis Dupré, "Spiritual Life in a Secular Age," *Daedelus*, Winter 1982, p. 25.
5. Kenneth Boulding, *There Is a Spirit: The Nayler Sonnets* (Madison, N.J.: The Golden Hind Press, 1975).

II. SCRIPTURAL RESOURCES

3. Social Transformation

JAMES A. FORBES, JR.

Everyone agrees that changes are needed in society as it exists today, but they do not agree on specifics like what kinds of changes, where and when they are to take place, who is to bear the expense, who are to be the leaders, and what is to be the ultimate end. Much of the discussion about the need for change is unfocused and insubstantial. Complaints and protests abound, but solid proposals for remedial action are usually lacking. Expressions of dissatisfaction may provide temporary relief of the symptoms of distress, but they hold no promise for new conditions. Conversations about social transformation really begin to be significant when the people discussing the issue speak specifically about the vision that inspires their hope; when they articulate the programmatic thrust they propose; and when they describe the source of power and sustenance that they are convinced is available to those who commit themselves to the implementation of world-changing plans. This is the quality of conversation intended in this chapter.

The vision that sparks my concern for societal change and focuses my understanding of the task comes from the Bible. I do not mean this in a simplistic Bible-verse-leaping-out-at-me-from-the-Holy-Book way, but as a perspective reflecting the general spirit of the biblical witness fundamental to the thinking of the Christian faith as I understand it and a conviction that the highest source of wisdom about how the world ought to be shaped is revealed in the pages of the Scriptures. Each age is required to receive the holy cues and discern contemporary meanings and mandates. Out of this analysis should come greater clarity about the changes needed and a willingness to dedicate time and resources in the service of the divinely inspired vision.

One of the most powerful images of the world-transforming work of God is found in Jeremiah 18:1–6:

> The word that came to Jeremiah from the Lord: "Arise, and go down to the potter's house, and there I will let you hear my words." So I went down to the potter's house, and there he was working at his wheel. And the vessel he was making of clay was spoiled in the potter's hand, and he reworked it into another vessel, as it seemed good to the potter to do. Then the word of the Lord came to me: "O House of Israel, can I not do with you as the potter has done?" says the Lord. "Behold, like the clay in the potter's hand, so you are in my hand, O House of Israel."

The faith basis for the social transformation I commend here is found in this passage. (Although the message was first addressed to the House of Israel, it is later extended to "any nation or kingdom" [18:7–10].)

Jeremiah observed the potter at work. What impressed him most was what happened when the vessel was marred in the potter's hand. Upon discovering the flaw, the potter mashed the marred vessel back into a lump of clay and began to make another vessel. The identification of God with the potter can be interpreted in the following way: The Creator had a design in mind; the covenant people failed to turn out as they were intended to, but like the potter, God is willing to start again to make another vessel that God can declare good. To respond in faithfulness requires a willingness to consent to the remaking process, based on the conviction that the God of creation still has a definite design in mind.

What kind of society did the Potter intend to shape? In what way was Israel to organize its life so that it could represent the divine intentions? Today those of us who are concerned with the crucial questions of social transformation from the Christian perspective are still in need of the understanding and vision, as well as a blueprint or outline, from the heart and mind of the first Potter.

In my seminary days we called such a design the "order of creation." It referred to some sense of how God ordered things from the beginning. The divine specifications provided clues to be followed in the contemporary reordering of our society. It is not easy to speak of such matters today. Where would we look anymore to recover intimations of what God had in mind at the dawn of creation? The critical spirit with which we approach the sources of theology today renders us less certain than our ancestors were in matters of faith and order. Nonetheless, it is part of the Christian vocation in every age to keep alive what we can recall or discern of the pattern the Potter had in mind, in order to serve that intention in the present.

Jeremiah claimed to have heard from the Lord indications both of what had gone wrong and what God still intended to make of the people called God's chosen. For him what the Potter had in mind was centered in the relationship between Israel and God. The fundamental flaw was that a rift had developed between the people and the God who created them. They offered incense to false gods and stumbled over detours and took shortcuts, neglecting the well-charted highways. The covenant relationship had been broken. The people had forgotten their God. They did not live as if their lives were rooted in the relationship to the God who called them into existence. When challenged with their unfaithfulness, they insisted that they would continue in the way that they had chosen.

All this is found in chapter 18 after the account of the observation at the potter's house. The fundamental flaw is that the people of the covenant had decided to seek their fulfillment apart from the conditions of the covenant relationship, apart from the God of creation. Everything Jeremiah condemned is related to that fundamental rift. No matter what people make of their lives, all the patterns, whether they be social, economic, or political, reflect the fundamental relationship from which they have developed the covenant that has defined their identity. Jeremiah keeps reminding the people that there is a break between the God of the covenant and the pattern of behavior of the nation. Oppression of the poor, unholy cultic practices, personal immorality—all these reflect the same fundamental flaw.

In the light of this theological understanding, we must focus our concern for social transformation at a deeper level than the necessary study of the nature of social systems and of various political philosophies. We must have some sense of the basic rift in the divine/human relationship, be willing to face it, and be willing to do whatever is necessary to fix it.

Let us return to Jeremiah. His troubled career reveals that

prophecy can be "injurious to one's health." Becoming seriously committed to hearing what the Potter had in mind can be the beginning of trouble. Once you claim to be a servant of the God who has observed a flaw in the vessel and give evidence of trying to engage in determined efforts to fix the flaw, certain consequences are inevitable. The nineteenth chapter of Jeremiah shows what is likely to happen to one who has been drawn into the pathos of God, one who cries out words of judgment in the face of resistance to God's remedial intentions. God tells Jeremiah:

Go, buy a potter's earthen flask, and take some of the elders of the people and some of the senior priests, and go out to the valley of the son of Hinnon at the entry of the Potsherd Gate, and proclaim there the words that I tell you. (vv. 1–2)

Then you shall break the flask in the sight of the men who go with you, and shall say to them, "Thus says the Lord of Hosts: So will I break this people and this city, as one breaks a potter's vessel, so that it can never be mended." (v. 11a)

God has a way of moving the committed from mere observation to solid participation in God's plans for restoration and repair. A person who becomes impressed by and extraordinarily committed to what God's design is will be called with prophetic urgency to translate God's design into a living reality. Observe the movement to tangibility, "Get a pot and proclaim my words." The Lord tells Jeremiah to read out the long list of the people's shortcomings, and once again it has to do with the broken relationship: The people have forsaken God, have profaned the holy place by burning incense to other gods, have filled this place with the blood of innocents, and have built the high places of Ba'al to burn their sons in the fire as burnt offerings. "Break the pot in the eyes of the people as a demonstration of my wrath and judgment."

As long as one just talks about God's great dream, one may be tolerated, but when one identifies overmuch with God's insistence on making another vessel, by mashing down or by the smashing of a vessel never to be mended again, serious repercussions are to be expected. When one describes Jeremiah's beautiful experience at the potter's house, it seems gentle, almost romantic—tender, loving hands shaping and reshaping. But what happens when the clay starts to set and harden? The image shifts from a gentle mashing of the clay to the crushing of the vessel.

The image of God as the potter intent on making another vessel sets the stage for the emergence of conflict. The "powers that be" in all generations have resisted God's gentle efforts to make things what they ought to be. The nature and scope of this resistance can be detected very early in the process of institutionalization. The nature of social systems and political philosophies tends toward the erection of barriers against reforms prophets urge as the mandate of God.

The movement from what is to what ought to be takes place on a path fraught with great peril. Those who dare to be fixers will discover that the word *fix* has more than one meaning. They "fixed" Jeremiah, placing him in the stocks to intimidate him into silence and acceptance of the status quo.

Before moving to further reflection on how Jeremiah's experience challenges us today, let us summarize several important factors to be considered in the planning of faith-based ministeries of transformation.

First, there should be the strong conviction that God has a design in mind to which God is still committed. If we believe that God has given up on us and has no further investment in the context in which we live, all our hopes are groundless.

Second, there must be confidence that the people of faith have been called to be instruments in revisioning and reshaping the larger society. Their relationship with God and their vocation in the world are part of the same pattern.

Third, there must be the expectation of ongoing divine disclosure of some basic ideas regarding what the reworked vessel will be like. It is likely that the new vision will be in continuity with the original intent and will include the traditional elements of shalom, justice, righteousness, Torah, and care for the oppressed. In every age, God's pattern will continue to be revealed through people within the community who have the gifts of vision and discernment.

Fourth, the community of faith, and especially the prophetic visionaries sent by God, must be prepared to be threatened and rejected by the guardians of the present social order. Entrenched interests and ongoing enterprises will usually regard any prophetic visions as an attack on their very essence, for example, their power relationships and profits.

Fifth, special consideration must be given to how servants of the divine potter are nurtured to maturity of faith, so that they can be sustained in faithful service even under conditions of stress and repression.

CHRISTIAN RESPONSIBILITY FOR SOCIAL TRANSFORMATION

With this general framework in mind, let us turn now to a Christian understanding of responsibility for social transformation. At the heart of the Christian faith is the affirmation that in Jesus we find the embodiment of what the Potter had in mind for us as individuals, as well as a description of the kind of design intended for the world. Amid the various Christologies is the underlying witness that the vessel the Potter seeks to make can best be viewed in the person of the Nazarene. To be like him in character, devotion, and faithfulness is to fulfill the dream of God.

But what of the society in which we are to live? Jesus announced that the Kingdom of God is at hand even in this society. The contours of the reign or rule of God were presented in parables and beatitudes and in the manner of his ministry among his disciples.

The multitude of those who attended to his teaching and witnessed his miracles were taught the Kingdom implications of the signs and wonders. The Sermon on the Mount and the sermon in his hometown synagogue sketch the features of the Kingdom. It is God's gift of Good News for the poor, God's affirmative action program, the liberating word to all sorts and conditions of broken humanity. It is rooted in God's unconditional love for all people, who are forgiven and redeemed by a God-given atoning grace. Human arrangements are reversed so that the last becomes first and the least becomes the greatest. Those who work for peace and justice and learn to lead their lives in service are assured of power and guidance to be the salt of the earth and the light of the world. The invitation to bear witness is a call to words and deeds of Kingdom commitment. One's vision of the

Kingdom provides the criteria by which society is evaluated. One invests time, talent, and influence to serve the process of societal transformation so that God's Kingdom will come on earth as it is in heaven. One prays for this end and works for its realization in concrete ways.

What has been said thus far could be considered no more than the rhetoric of faith. The critical difference rests with those who, like Jeremiah, move beyond mere talk to demonstrations, people who participate in transformation. For them, general principles are translated into specific contemporary objectives. Thus movement toward the Kingdom calls for a serious pursuit of peace. Militarism must be overcome. Racism must be eliminated from the face of the earth, beginning with the present moment. Class exploitation, labeled as demonic, is therefore, unacceptable in human history. Sexism, ageism, hedonism, and materialism become issues for serious analysis and programmatic response, with long-term strategy formation.

Even this enumeration of pressing issues will mean very little unless people rise above mere slogans to program development. Serious programs with active participants, regular meeting places and meeting times, timetables for launching the offensive, and task forces for adequate follow-up are essential.

There is a great deal that committed people can do out of their own insights and resources. But thorough planning and judicious use of resources may not be enough. Beyond mobilization of human resources is the necessity for watching and waiting for the times and seasons of special promptings for resolute action. Such promptings may come as a clear discernment of the divine moment, or they may come in reaction to sinister forces escalating their evil schemes to the extent that nonresponse makes one an unwitting accomplice.

What is the community of faith called to do? An important first action, an important first consideration toward action, is recognition of the nature of the context in which we are called to serve. The wisdom from the potter's house urges the facing of flaws in the vessel, but there are strong forces working against honest facing of defects in ourselves and our society. We all know the natural tendency to avoid exposure of our imperfections. No one welcomes judgment or condemnation. This tendency works on the societal level as well. We are a cover-up people. Flaws are likely to be whitewashed or shellacked. Defective vessels are likely to be sold as antiques. But self-deception is hazardous indeed. Some of the major tragedies of our times resulted from the denial of defects. Buildings collapse, bridges fall, airplanes crash, and families and communities disintegrate. Even if certain interests appear to be served by masking the disturbing truth, the Church knows that deception and death are causally related.

The religious community must be unalterably committed to telling the truth about the society in which it exists. It must seek the truth and speak the truth. It must refuse to accept propaganda or scapegoating analysis. It must face and tell the truth about itself as an institution as it offers its critique of the larger social context. If the truth is consistently told, the Church will automatically discover a second part of its responsibility in preparation for action.

Agents of social transformation will need to cultivate an awareness of the inevitability of conflict. God's ways are not our ways. The Kingdom of God makes demands that undermine the dehumanizing values of the kingdom of this world. We are in the world but not of it. Thus we are in the middle of a tug-of-war. When we find ourselves thriving in easy conformity to prevailing trends, it is high time to do an oppression analysis. Without having deliberately compromised our values, we all have become beneficiaries of the system whose operating principles and practices are judged harshly by the basic tenets of our faith. For all our condemnation of principalities and powers, we unwittingly maintain respect for and loyalty to them in exchange for the security we derive from their network. Because of this strange and subtle alliance, people of faith must build into their personal and corporate understanding the need for self-criticism, confession, and repeated withdrawal from compromising partnerships and the dependencies they imply.

The gospel calls us to count up the cost of our witness. Part of this process is the assessing of our power as well. In God's grace the Church discovers that its members are not helpless victims of alien powers but bearers of gifts, competencies, and influence for effecting change. Just as Moses was told to use the rod in his hand and the disciples were bidden to feed the multitude with the lunch they had, so we are expected to use what we have. One of the functions of the Church is to help its members discover and release their power in ways that promote the cause of the Kingdom. Professionals and nonprofessionals, trained and untrained workers, rich and poor—all are influencing their context either by reinforcing the status quo or promoting change. The issue is not simply one of getting power but of becoming aware of how we use the power we have, and then developing expertise to make an impact on our communities for good. The Church is the sleeping giant. What a powerful witness we could be if the parts of the body came to a new awareness of the power that is at work within and around us!

Let us turn now to the action stage in the ministry of social transformation.

Proclamation is also action. Although this task is not usually the responsibility of the social action committee, it is a primary means by which the Church acts in the world in a transforming way. It is by the preaching of the word that the Church is saved and equipped for its liberating activity. If the preaching does not make a difference in the shape of the world, it is a defective form of communication. Jesus preached and Nazareth was never the same again. Peter preached and a new social arrangement emerged in the New Testament community. Paul preached and exploitative business practices were effectively challenged. This is action, and the Church must not forget the impact of preachers through the ages whose proclamation made the difference in slavery, women's rights, industrial relations, the pursuit of peace, and the very means of production.

Preaching that sparks change dares to correlate the vision of the Bible with the various arenas of contemporary human activity. Thereby it avoids the trivialization of the gospel, which occurs when the eschatological vision seems indifferent to the hungers, hurts, doubts, and fears of the people who walk in darkness on our city streets. For example, let us look at the vision of John at the end of the Book of Revelation, which gives a picture of the heavenly city. Although it may be preached as a symbolic representation of the way things will be at the end, the preacher's task can also be to show how the splendor of the end is also insinuated in the world today. Without collapsing the anticipatory expression of hope for the future into presumed fulfillment in the present, the preacher can help the hearers to discern hints of heaven in the here and now and provide orientation and direction to our action.

Then he showed me the river of the water of life, bright as crystal, flowing from the throne of God and of the Lamb through the middle of the street of the city; also on either side of the river, the tree of life with its twelve kinds of fruit, yielding its fruit each month: and the leaves of the tree were for the healing of the nations. There shall no more be anything accursed, but the throne of God and of the Lamb shall be in it and his servants shall worship him; they shall see his face, and his name shall be on their foreheads. And night shall be no more; they need no light of lamp or sun, for the Lord God will be their light, and they shall reign for ever and ever. (Rev. 22:1–5)

This vision describes the kind of world the Potter is designing and provides the orientation and direction for faithful action: *The river of the water of life, bright as crystal* speaks of life, integrity, and ecological purity. *The tree of life on either side of the river* suggests beauty and growth on both sides of the town. *Twelve kinds of fruit each month* suggests a world without hunger. *Leaves on the tree for the healing of the nations* speaks of peace among the nations and provisions for the health of all the people. *God's name on their foreheads* points out to us respect for all people, who are to be viewed as "hand-made by God."

With this vision firmly in mind and deeply rooted in the heart, one sets about the work of bearing witness in deed. The way one votes, invests resources, organizes one's life, makes a living, and serves the community will intentionally incline toward the vision. Beyond what individuals do on their own there is a responsibility for the religious community as a body. Local, regional, national, and international expressions of the Church provide different levels on which to serve in the quest for a better world. Ecumenical and interfaith cooperation is mandated as evidence of good stewardship of opportunities. Meanwhile, advocacy relationships may be established with secular enterprises, or watchdog organizations may be used to hold the system accountable. Although it is impossible to participate in every venture, each community must prayerfully determine what the limits are for direct action as well as for financial and moral support.

Some form of deliberate decision making ought to take place regarding social transformation in all religious communities. The discussion ought to include at least the following questions:

1. What is our vision of what God wills for the world?
2. Where is this vision most clearly revealed in Scripture?
3. Where do we have evidence of God's power bringing about change?
4. What are the forces at work against the emerging vision?
5. What power in our midst is available for the work of transformation?
6. In what ways does our community participate in blocking the Kingdom's advance?
7. To what specific activities do we feel especially called in service of the good?
8. How may we support others who are involved in different aspects of this task?
9. What is the cost of attempting to be God's agents of change in our situation?
10. Are we ready to pay the price?

Consideration of these issues should prepare a church to organize and mobilize for action. There is no action package appropriate for all situations. The quality of the action is stronger when it grows out of the reflection/research/resolve of those who are expected to implement specific programs. Some churches will specialize in acts of charity; others will feel called to change systems, like reversing patterns of racial or sexual discrimination or challenging unjust aspects of the economic system. Still others will build new experiments or Kingdom demonstration projects, like intentional communities, communal industrial projects, or basic human services cooperatives.

The ministry of Dr. Martin Luther King, Jr., serves me as a model for the Christian response to the need for social transformation. He stood in the Jeremiah tradition. Not only did he have a dream, but he was also empowered to transform that dream into demonstrative expressions of divine urgency to make things change. One may have a profusion of dreams, and even broadcast them, without making a difference. It is the movement of transformative action that is likely to provoke violent resistance. Dr. King was willing to face the flaw in our nation and world, and he invested his gifts in fixing what had gone wrong.

As a young man living in Atlanta, Georgia, King saw an alien blotch, a black spot on the vessel of his community. A black spot on the vessel symbolizes racism. Young King could not eat in the downtown lunch counters. In addition to this humiliation, he also observed the rift between the classes. As he broadened his understanding through education, he saw more clearly the link between race and class discrimination. Thus, the flaw was more than a black spot. It ran throughout the society and threatened the quality of human existence on a worldwide scale. Prayerfully and in community, he led the nonviolent resistance movement against segregation.

King later came to see the interrelatedness of race, class, and military and economic intervention in the international arena. He discovered the fundamental flaw in the tendency of human beings to secure themselves, to promote their own personal interests at the expense of others. Thus he broadened his focus beyond civil rights issues and dared to speak out against the war in Vietnam. Some people, in lamenting his tragic assassination, felt that if he had only stuck to black/white issues, his life might have been spared. Criticizing the war was off limits.

Was that really the unpardonable sin? It seems that Dr. King was really on the verge of telling the truth about our society in a way in which we were not accustomed to hearing it. He discovered that the beloved community that God had in mind was not going to arise out of our system as it was presently organized and operating. Although I have no evidence that King was prepared to propose a radically new system, all indications are that he had become convinced that this nation could not fulfill its promise to God or humanity, apart from radical reordering, mashing down, closing down, of our system for in-depth and long overdue renovation. He was convinced that a major intervention in the political life of the nation was the only thing that could get the job done. Big plans, therefore, were in the making for confronting the nation in a more serious demonstration than the others he had led. This would not be a cheery, "We shall overcome" get-together but a major effort to end the dehumanizing pattern of our ongoing social, economic, and political way of life and to orient the country toward a serious redirection of resources and power internally. King had become ready to join the Jeremiah tradition. Through nonviolent demonstrations in the nation's capital, he intended to confront our leaders with the fact that there is a fundamental flaw in the way the system is organized.

As long as we keep our investment in militarism, classism, racism, and illicit interference in the affairs of other nations, we will not be able to fulfill the American dream of equality, liberty, and justice. King knew the cost of such a challenge. He understood what happened to Jeremiah. As long as Jeremiah stuck to talking, they considered him to be an annoying presence. But when he took the flask and shattered it and said, "This is what the Lord is going to do with us," the authorities came to the conclusion that this man was an unbearable threat to the stability of the nation. He must be silenced or eliminated. Such a judgment was also made of King as his impact on the conscience of the nation came to be perceived as threat rather than promise.

The example of Martin Luther King shows that if we dare to do more than just complain and actually go on to mobilize moral and spiritual force to narrow the gap between what the Potter has in mind and the way the world is shaped, it could be injurious to our health. If we move from mere speaking to a real willingness to fix the flaw, we are reminded that we ourselves will be "fixed." When one is involved in in-depth social transformation, one had better count up the cost in advance of the action.

No matter what social transformation activities are chosen, there must be vigilance lest other dimensions of the Church's mission be neglected. Issues of personal salvation, maintenance of hope and encouragement in the face of struggle, and concern for cultural and social uplift will remain perennial priorities along with action. Without them no action movement can survive; its members will burn out.

Dr. Martin Luther King, Jr., told of the growing strain he had to bear as he found himself serving as an instrument of mashing down and rebuilding. He spoke of receiving threatening phone calls all through the night, having his children harassed, his house bombed. He finally had had enough and decided that it was time to end his leadership of the movement. How moving it is to hear of the night he came to the end of his strength. He got up from bed and went into the kitchen to prepare some coffee. He sat with his head in his hands and told the Lord that he couldn't go any further; he had done all he could. And yet a conversation took place between King and the Lord in which King was reassured that the Lord would indeed be with him and his efforts would not be in vain. From such a moment of profound encouragement, he resumed his leadership with new confidence and determination.

The question raised is this: How are persons of faith formed so that they will serve the vision of the Potter and experience the force of God's word within themselves as strong enough to withstand the pressures from the outside? I am convinced that sustained dedication to social transformation calls for a more radical implanting of the vision deep within, so that it is, in the words of Jeremiah, "shut up in my bones."

Christians will think of Jesus as the fixer par excellence. The gospel record makes it clear that he was always sensitive to the distance between how things were in his time and what the Potter had in mind from the beginning. His whole ministry may be viewed as a massive reshaping project, on both the individual and social levels. The fallen creation is touched by the hands of one who bore in his own being the design the Potter dreamed. Through his teaching, healing, reconciling, dying, and rising, a new vessel is being shaped. The disciples are apprentices in the process of transformation. Let us turn now to examine that process in greater detail.

SPIRITUAL FORMATION FOR SOCIAL TRANSFORMATION

We can now speak about the kind of Church capable of doing what must be done to make the witness effective. It should be acknowledged that the Church generally does not function in accordance with the pattern described. When we ask why there is discontinuity between principles and practice, we find that the explanation must somehow relate to the nature of the formation of the members. The task calls for people who are Kingdom-conscious and willing to serve the Kingdom in spite of the price and the risk to their security. The mandate of the Lord should constitute a compelling force. The threat of reprisal or persecution, although taken seriously, does not force retreat from faithfulness to the divine agenda. A Church comprising such people will make a difference in the world.

The disciples of Jesus and the members of the early Church, although they were not perfect, are role models for the kind of people we have described. It should be instructive for us to take a fresh look at how they came to commit themselves to the task of facing and fixing the flaws.

At the heart of their formation is Jesus, the Christ, insofar as he embodies the vision of the Potter and releases people from the need to deny or overlook the flaws in the social context. A relationship to him is crucial; it is not only his teachings, methods, or models that must be learned and then implemented. The disciples were reminded:

Abide in me, and I in you. As the branch cannot bear fruit by itself, unless it abides in the vine, neither can you, unless you abide in me. I am the vine, you are the branches . . . for apart from me, you can do nothing. (John 15:4–5)

There are a number of interpretations of how one is to center one's witness and work in Christ. No effort will be made here to distinguish between the various formulations of how we abide in the presence. The real point is that a foundational connection with the Lord of the Christian faith is presupposed when there is any discussion of fulfilling Christian ministry. The disciples are called, and they respond by joining themselves to Jesus. The nurturing process begins.

The preparation of the apostles for their work began with the formation of a Kingdom-conscious community. Although individuals may have been recruited singly or in pairs, it was as a community of learners that they were equipped for the ministry. In the school of discipleship, Jesus shared with them intimate details about his own emerging sense of who he was and what he must do to accomplish the work of the one who had sent him.

There was instruction regarding the nature of the Kingdom of Heaven that Jesus said was at hand. The tradition was reviewed so as to discern the depths to which it pointed or to identify the elements of it that had become distorted. Prayer together oriented their hearts and minds toward the God above, whose good pleasure it was both to send the Kingdom and to empower them to be servants of the new era that was dawning.

Beyond prayer and reflection there was action. Life in the community was a living laboratory of liberating activity. Acts of compassion manifested the power of God, and challenges of reigning tradition highlighted the authority from which Jesus acted. What they encountered in the course of a day was reviewed and criticized in the more intimate circles of the disciples when they retreated from the crowds. Such was their college of Christian formation. (See Mark, chapter 4, for an exciting day of learning with the Teacher.)

If we find it impossible to sustain the transforming witness in our time, we may need to compare our process of nurture with theirs:

1. Is there a real sense of what it means to have a living relationship with the resurrected Lord?
2. Is it only religious jargon to talk of Christ being in the midst of us where two or three are gathered?
3. Can most Christians today pass a test on the basic meanings of the Kingdom of God?
4. What is the level of experiential investment in the Kingdom of God coming on earth as it is in heaven?
5. Do our prayers predispose us, not only to trust God for our survival, but also to become God's agents of emergency care for those who are scattered like sheep without a shepherd?
6. Do most of our churches provide a contest for Kingdom-conscious reflection-in-faith as members wrestle with principalities and powers or seek to cope with sundry assaults against their faith?
7. Are we in the habit of recording and celebrating occurrences that point to the overcoming power of God and demonstrate God's authority over all usurping forces in our society?

We will continue to be frustrated about the powerlessness of the Church until we pay more attention to the process by which our Lord prepared those who went out to turn the world upside down.

Another dimension of spiritual formation is highlighted in the New Testament Church. According to Luke 24:44–49, Jesus, in a postresurrection appearance to the disciples, summarized his teachings but then went on to urge them to await an additional experience of preparation:

And behold, I send the promise of my father upon you; but stay in the city until you are clothed with power from on high. (Luke 24:49)

The Book of Acts records what happened to those who assembled to pray and await the promise. The descent of the Holy Spirit on the day of Pentecost marks the birthday of the Church. Amid various understandings of what actually happened that day there emerges the unanimous testimony that the power to be the Church depends upon the presence of the Holy Spirit. Jesus had promised the disciples:

But you shall receive power when the Holy Spirit has come upon you; and you shall be my witnesses in Jerusalem and all Judea and Samaria and to the end of the earth. (Acts 1:8)

That they needed to wait for the Spirit before launching out upon their assignment leaves no doubt that the Spirit is absolutely essential for the work of the Church.

The spectacular features of the account of the coming of the Spirit in chapter 2 of Acts, tongues of fire, rushing mighty wind, and tongues of ecstasy, signal the guiding and empowering presence of God. Peter's sermon identifies the Pentecostal happening as the fulfillment of Joel's prophecy:

And in the last days if shall be, God declares, that I will pour out my Spirit upon all flesh, and your young men shall see visions, and your old men shall dream dreams; yea, and on my menservants and my maidservants in those days I will pour out my Spirit; and they shall prophesy. (Acts 2:17-18)

Thus the Church was released for its mission when its members learned through experience that God's power was indeed with them. In the light of that assurance, they went forth with courage to live out the witness for which they had been called, instructed, and equipped with power.

The transforming power of the Holy Spirit experience is reflected in the boldness and effectiveness of Peter's preaching after the encounter in the Upper Room. He overcame the tendency to play it safe. He no longer yielded to the temptation to put his security above everything else, as he had done when confronted by the young damsel, at the time of Jesus' trial. Now he could be depended upon to speak the word of truth without inordinate regard for the possibility of negative repercussions. But an even more remarkable evidence of the transforming power of the experience of Pentecost was the formation of a community with such trust in God that they were willing to share their resources according to each other's need:

And all who believed were together and had all things in common: and they sold their possessions and goods and distributed them to all, as any had need. (Acts 2:44–45)

There are several qualifications one can make about the extent to which this description reflected the actual norm of the Church and to what extent and for how long this was practiced. Nevertheless we must take the account as a serious indication that contact with the Holy Spirit produced a community with a greater willingness to share than was usual.

In the early Church other impressive signs of spiritual maturity and openness to the Spirit can be found. When the Hellenists murmured against the Hebrews because their widows were being neglected in the distribution of the daily rations, the leadership gracefully responded by setting up a structure to assure fairness (Acts 6:6). It is interesting to note that the names of the people chosen to administer the program were members of the *aggrieved* part of the community. Consider also the way the Spirit was able to lead Peter and his companions to overcome their prejudices against the Gentiles. The experience of the Spirit was so vivid and powerful that previous perceptions and practices gave way to the unfolding wisdom of the Spirit (Acts 10:44–48).

Acts 15 presents a classic example of how the Holy Spirit aided the Church in its effort to clear up a major social/spiritual problem. Circumcision was a powerful issue that threatened the unity of the Church. The question of whether the Gentiles should be circumcised was so volatile a controversy that a gathering of the leadership of the Church had to be convened to deal with the matter. There was heated discussion on each side of the issue, but the tangible sense of the consulting presence of the Spirit enabled them to reach an acceptable resolution of the problem. Their memo of conciliation begins with these words: "For it seemed good to the Holy Spirit and to us to lay upon you no greater burden than these necessary things . . . " (Acts 15:28).

It was the openness to the Spirit's agenda and the willingness to let go of cherished self-perceptions and securities that made the Church such a powerful instrument for change. Ability to consent to the divine/human collaboration generated a force felt beyond the circle of believers. Thus it was said of two companions of the Christian community, albeit with exaggerated claims, "These men who have turned the world upside down have come here also" (Acts 17:6).

The magnitude of the problems needing to be addressed in our time should incline us to acknowledge that the Church could scarcely aspire to have significant impact without a fresh empowerment of the Spirit. Biblical understanding assures us that Pentecost was an event that need not be repeated. Yet there is the urgent need for the Church to learn how to appropriate the dynamic of power and vision so that we need not approach our work with mere human strength.

Spiritual formation for our time calls for in-depth training in Kingdom understanding and the cultivation of a keen sense of the presence and power of the Spirit. When the Church learns how to provide a program of Christian nurture that can make both these elements come alive, we, its people, will more frequently reflect the courage, conviction, and power necessary to face and fix the flaws in our society.

As we approach the year 2000, how fitting it would be for the Church to do a fresh analysis of the flaws marring the wholeness to which we have been called in Christ. At least we should be able to name the defects in the created order. It may even be time to launch a massive recall of Christians to have the Potter mend or renew in us all that is less than God intended. As we are renewed as a community of faith, we should go forth as agents of transformation so that the flaws of the twentieth century will not be the unfinished business preventing us from facing the emerging agenda of a new millennium.

4. Lectio Divina: Receiving the Revelation

M. BASIL PENNINGTON, O.C.S.O.

The title of this book is a rather awesome one; it raises many questions. What is a time of apocalypse? Do we live in such a time? What is social compassion? Do I have it? What are the spiritual resources I draw upon?

As I began to reflect on this, I realized that a shift had taken place in my own consciousness. Sometime within the last year or two—I cannot pinpoint the time—the context of my thinking had changed. I had begun to view life and everything I did with the realization that at any moment this civilization as we know it, if not the entire globe, could come promptly to an end.

This, of course, has always been factually true and a clear part of the Revelation. According to the Gospels, our Lord in the last days of his life spoke prophetically of the end times. In response to the query of his disciples: "Tell us . . . what will be the sign of your coming and of the end of the world?" Jesus replied:

You will hear of wars and rumors of wars . . . nation will fight against nation, and kingdom against kingdom. There will be famines and earthquakes here and there . . . the sun will be darkened, the moon will lose its brightness, the stars will fall from the sky and the powers of heaven will be shaken. And then the sign of the Son of Man will appear in heaven. (Matthew 24)

The early Christians accepted this coming of Christ with the ending of the world as imminent; it colored all their thinking and actions. But as the years followed one after another, the sense of imminence waned.

Today there is a revival of this sense, and with good reason. The many signs our Lord spoke of are more than abundantly present. In addition, we are literally surrounded by powerfully destructive nuclear warheads, poised to wreak such havoc over vast surfaces of the face of the earth that those who survive will envy the dead while they await the extinction of all life as the fallout relentlessly pervades the whole atmosphere.

I was startled and deeply affected recently when at the daily Liturgy the lector read a passage from Saint Peter's Second Letter. I had undoubtedly heard it many times before and had even read it myself more than once. But now I heard it in a new context and heard in it a powerful prophecy of nuclear destruction:

The present sky and earth are destined for fire. . . . The Day of the Lord will come like a thief, and then with a roar the sky will vanish, the elements will catch fire and fall apart, the earth and all that it contains will be burnt up. Since everything is coming to an end like this, you should be living holy and saintly lives while you wait and long for the Day of God to come, when the sky will dissolve in flames and the elements melt in the heat. (2 Pet. 3:7–12)

This certainly sounds like a nuclear holocaust.

In our fear and in hope, we are apt to run back to early pages of the same holy text when Yahweh saw that the wickedness of man was great on the earth and that the thoughts in his heart fashioned nothing but wickedness all day long. Yahweh regretted having made man on the earth, and his heart grieved, "I will rid the earth's face of man, my own creation," Yahweh said, "and of animals also, reptiles too, and the birds of heaven: for I regret having made them" (Gen. 6:5–7).

"But Noah had found favor with Yahweh. . . . Noah was a good man" (Gen. 6:8–9). In fact, he was a most remarkable man. He truly believed God and acted on faith. And his faith saved us all. He lived to see his home and the land he loved totally devastated. Yet this "man of integrity" who "walked with God"—this innocent man—emerged from his months of imprisonment in the ark and immediately turned to God in worship and thanksgiving. In response to such goodness, God responded: "Never again will I curse the earth. . . . Never again will I strike down every living thing as I have done. As long as earth lasts, sowing and reaping, cold and heat, summer and winter, day and night shall cease no more" (Gen. 8:21–22).

We seek to draw hope from this promise of Yahweh. Yet we must remember that the word *apocalypsis* means an "uncovering." Saint Peter speaks in this context: "What we are waiting for is what he promised: the new heavens and the new earth, the place where righteousness will be at home" (2 Pet. 3:13). There is hope even beyond apocalypse, beyond nuclear holocaust. This does not mean we should not strive with all the means at our command for total disarmament, nuclear and otherwise, for peace in all its fullness. "Blessed are the peacemakers, for they shall be called the children of God" (Matt. 5:9). Even as we strive for peace and disarmament, Saint Peter gives us a course of action: "So then, my friends, while you are waiting, do your best to live lives without spot or stain so that he will find you at peace" (2 Pet. 3:14). Peace must begin within our own hearts. A heart torn by the violence of sin and hatred will never create peace. "You have been warned about this, my friends; be careful not to get carried away by the errors of unprincipled people from the firm ground that you are standing on" (2 Pet. 3:17). Deterrence, fear, threat, can never be the firm ground of peace; they are unprincipled. The violence that they incarnate can in the end only erupt and be part of the devastation of the earth. "Instead, go on growing in the grace and in the knowledge of our Lord Jesus Christ" (2 Pet. 3:18).

Herein lies my answer to the question of or search for spiritual resources for social compassion in a time of apocalypse: *in the knowledge of our Lord Jesus Christ.* My answer is necessarily a simple one, "Be simple as doves ['Unless you become as little ones you will not enter in' (Matt. 18:3)]," yet a powerful one, "and wise as serpents" (Matt. 10:16). Simplicity cuts right through to the heart of things. "The word of God is something alive and active: it cuts like any two-edged sword but more finely, it can slip through the place where the soul is divided from the spirit, or joints from the marrow; it can judge the secret emotions and thoughts" (Heb. 4:12).

Along with our Jewish (and Moslem) brothers and sisters, we have the privilege of being sons and daughters of the Book, recipients of the revelation. God has spoken to us. He has given us his all-powerful, healing, and comforting Word. This Word is our spiritual resource for social compassion in a time of apocalypse. Or, more precisely, it is the manifestation of and the way to the ultimate source: the all-merciful and compassionate heart of God our Father.

My response is an essentially Christian one, for I am a disciple of Christ, who came to reveal to us the love of the Father, the Father of Love. "No one knows the Father except the Son, and those to whom the Son chooses to reveal him" (Matt. 11:27). I realize some of my readers may not be Christians. May my response then invite them to consider taking Christ as their Master, or at least to reconsider their own tradition in the light of Christ.

The Christian tradition since the earliest days of the Latin Fathers has spoken of *lectio divina*. It would not do to simply translate this consecrated phrase, "divine reading." First of all, when we use the expression *lectio* in this traditional sense, we are always using it in the context of a whole process: *lectio, meditatio, oratio,* and *contemplatio.* Secondly, it could not mean simply "reading," because a large segment of the Christian community through many centuries could not read.

Lectio here means, rather, receiving the revelation. Certainly, for most of us today this will most often take place through personal reading—the time we spend with the Holy Scriptures, listening to the Word of God. In times past, the revelation came more through hearing. Even today the most privileged moment of receiving the revelation is when we are gathered as Christian community at the Liturgy and the Gospel is proclaimed. As the Second Vatican Council taught in its *Constitution on the Sacred Liturgy,* when the Gospel is read at Mass, Christ again proclaims his Good News.

Have you ever noticed how this is brought out in the Liturgy of formal liturgical traditions? The Liturgy is a great teacher if we are attentive. As the moment for the Gospel approaches, the priest or the deacon rises and greets the people: "The Lord be with you." We respond: "And also with you." Then the priest says: "The Holy Gospel according to Saint . . . " And what do we reply? "Glory to you, Lord." It is as though the priest disappeared and the Lord Jesus now stands there. And at the end: "Praise to you, Lord Jesus Christ." The priest ceases to be, and Jesus Christ proclaims his Good News.

In earlier days, people seemed to have better developed memories. It was not uncommon for the faithful to retain in their memories much of the Gospels, as well as other parts of the Scriptures. It has been said of Saint Bernard of Clairvaux and of others that they knew the whole Bible by heart. *Lectio* then could be hearing the Word again recounted by one's own memory. The revelation also invited a hearing in the frescoes and icons, and later in the stained glass windows. The whole Bible can be found in the windows of the cathedral at Chartres. Preachers broke the Word open for the people. And there was simple faith sharing among friends, neighbors, and travelers or co-workers. Indeed, we have but to open our eyes to have God reveal himself to us. Saint Bernard found God "more in the trees and in the brooks than in the books." Creation in countless ways speaks of God and his love from sunrise to sunset and the midnight stars and the man in the moon. Nowhere is God so revealed as in the eyes of a beloved. Every human is a pre-eminent sacrament of him in whose image we are made.

All life, then, can be *lectio,* a revelation of God's loving presence and care. I would, though, at this point, like to share with you a very practical and simple method for doing *lectio divina.* If we consecrate a few minutes each day specifically to *lectio,* to receiving the revelation, it will form in us an attitude that can then spread to the rest of the day and transform our whole attitude toward life, toward everyone and everything. This very simple method is based on our monastic tradition and practice as it is presented in our *Book of Usages.* It goes back many, many centuries.

1. *Come into the Presence and call upon the Spirit.* The monastic regulations say that when a monk or nun is about to begin *lectio* he or she takes up the Sacred Text, kneels, calls upon the Holy Spirit, and listens to the first verse on his or her knees. He or she then kisses the text. What we want to emphasize here is the real Presence. God is truly present in his inspired Word. This is brought out in monastic churches, where we find two lamps always burning: one before the tabernacle proclaiming the real Presence of Christ in the Holy Eucharist and another over the enthroned Bible proclaiming his real Presence in the Sacred Text. He is present, ready to speak to us. Our Bible should never

be treated as just another book, thrown on the desk or shelved with other books. It should be enthroned in our room or office. We take it up with reverence and in some way acknowledge God's special Presence in it. A full, incarnated recognition involving the body is more appropriate—befitting us as incarnate persons—and more effective. We come, then, into his Presence and call upon the Spirit. It is the Holy Spirit who inspired and guided the sacred writers. It is the Holy Spirit who dwells in us to teach us: "The Advocate, the Holy Spirit, whom the Father will send in my name, will teach you everything and remind you of all I have said to you" (John 14:26). We rely on him to make the revealed Word come alive in us.

2. *Listen for ten or fifteen minutes.* Note, I say "listen," not "read." God is present. We listen to him. If he speaks to us powerfully in the first word or sentence, we stay with him, we respond. We listen and let him speak to us in whatever way he wants—through the words or between the lines. "Speak, Lord, your servant is listening" (1 Sam. 3:10).

We listen for ten or fifteen minutes or more. Set your own time. The monk or nun usually listens till the next bell rings. You have to create your own time spaces. But do it by time. We have been so schooled to speed-reading that, if we plan on doing a paragraph or a page, we will be under compulsion until we complete the assigned amount. It is better if we can settle down for ten minutes, with no concern for covering an allotted text. We open ourselves to hear—in a word, a sentence, a paragraph, or a page. Who is too busy to make ten minutes a day to listen to the Master? If you are too busy for that, then you do really need to step back and examine your priorities. How can we say we are disciples of Christ if we will not give him even ten minutes a day to teach us the Way of Life?

3. *Thank God and take a word.* At the end of our allotted time, we want to thank God for being with us. It is a way of again acknowledging the real Presence. We are indeed privileged that God himself is willing, any time we wish, to come and sit down and speak to us. "I no longer call you servants, but friends, because I make known to you all that the Father has made known to me" (John 15:15). To get time with the bishop or the president of our company we have to go through all sorts of protocol,

set up appointments, and so forth. Not so with Almighty God! Thank him.

And take a word. If each day as we do our *lectio* one word, one idea, one insight, of his becomes ours, we will quickly come to have the mind of Christ. "Let this mind be in you which is in Christ Jesus" (Phil. 2:5). Some days the Lord will powerfully speak a word to us. It will echo in our being and perhaps be there forever. As I reflect now, I can remember a "word" he spoke thirty years ago.

More recently he spoke a "word" to me that has gained me a novel reputation. I am told that at a synod meeting the preacher referred to me as the "begot, begot mystic." He was retelling an experience that I had told him about. I was doing my *lectio,* listening to the opening verses of Saint Matthew's Gospel: "Abraham begot Isaac, Isaac begot Jacob, Jacob begot Judah . . ." I stopped the Lord, "Really now, Lord, I know you are a Jew and all this generation stuff may mean a lot to you, but what are you trying to say to me?" He answered, "Read on." And so on I went: "Obed begot Jesse, Jesse begot David, David begot Solomon. . . ." I said, "Lord, please, what are you trying to say?" He replied again, "Read on." And so I went on through three times fourteen generations till "Jacob begot Joseph, the husband of Mary, from whom was born Jesus. . . ." And at that moment I knew, as I never knew before and in a way that has never left me, that God *did* become man. He really took on *my humanity.* We are one in the same human flesh. God and I are human!

I had heard that Gospel how many times before? We used to read it at Vigils and Mass on many of the feasts of Blessed Mary. I had read it many times before in the course of my *lectio.* But that day, he spoke it. And *I heard.*

Some days at *lectio* the Lord seems very silent, very absent. We listen and listen—and seem to hear nothing. It is on such days that at the end of our *lectio* we have to choose a "word." We take a word, a phrase, a sentence, and carry it through the day. More often than not, we will find before the day is over it will come alive for us. Perhaps it will be during a conversation with someone or while we are reading something else, or while we are walking down the street.

There is a favorite passage of mine in one of the Easter sermons of Guerric of Igny, a twelfth-century Cistercian abbot. He is speaking to his monks about the three women who went to anoint Jesus' body. They found the tomb empty. As they began to retrace their steps, they met Jesus on the garden path. Guerric says to his monks: You know how it is, my brothers. Some days you go to your *lectio*, and the Lord is not there. You go to the prayer service, and the Lord is not there. You go to the Liturgy, the tomb of the altar, and the Lord is not there. Then you start off to work and, lo, halfway down the garden path you meet the Lord.

We take from our *lectio* a word of life and carry it with us through the day. This is the beginning of *meditatio*. I do not like to use the English word "meditation" here. In recent Christian usage it has come to mean doing a lot of thinking and analyzing along with some imaging, all according to one or another method. Today, more popularly, meditation refers to a sort of silent presence or a method to induce inner silence and transcendent experience. In early Christian tradition meditation meant neither of these directly. Rather, it was a simple repetition of the "word" received from *lectio* or from a spiritual father or mother. The "word" was repeated in the mind, or even on the lips, until it formed the heart and gave birth to *oratio*, "prayer," and *contemplatio*, "contemplation": a particular response, according to the word, or the silent response of one's whole being. "Be still and know that I am God" (Ps. 46:10).

The Fathers would illustrate such a process by pointing to the cow. The cow goes out and eats some good grass (*lectio*), then she sits down under a tree and chews her cud (*meditatio*) until she extracts from her food both milk (*oratio*) and cream (*contemplatio*).

Here we have then the most basic and traditional school of Christian spirituality: We receive the Word of God, his revelation, assimilate it, and respond to it. We receive the Word with a notional assent and allow it to form our mind and heart until there is a real assent, our whole being saying, "Yes, that's it."

I think we can readily see how this practice of *lectio*, taken in its full sense, is a powerful source for social compassion even in a time weighed heavily by a sense of apocalypse.

Receiving the revelation (*lectio*) we have a powerful source for hope. If Christ reveals anything, it is our Father's constant and most loving care:

That is why I am telling you not to worry about your life and what you are to eat, nor about your body and how you are to clothe it. Surely life means more than food, and the body more than clothing! Look at the birds in the sky. They do not sow or reap or gather into barns; yet your heavenly Father feeds them. Are you not worth much more than they are? Can any of you, for all his worrying, add one single cubit to his span of life? And why worry about clothing? Think of the flowers growing in the fields; they never have to work or spin; yet I assure you that not even Solomon in all his regalia was robed like one of these. Now if that is how God clothes the grass in the field which is there today and thrown into the furnace tomorrow, will he not much more look after you, you men of little faith? So do not worry; do not say, "What are we to eat? What are we to drink? How are we to be clothed?" It is the pagans who set their hearts on these things. Your heavenly Father knows you need them all. Set your hearts on his kingdom first, and on his righteousness, and all these other things will be given you as well. So do not worry about tomorrow: tomorrow will take care of itself. Each day has enough trouble of its own. (Matt. 6:25–34)

He who made this world at a word (Genesis 1) should be able to preserve it or, if he lets us use our freedom to destroy it, to remake it. He who prayed, "Father, forgive them, they do not know what they are doing" (Luke 23:34), and wills not the death of the sinner but that he turn and be saved (Ezek. 33:11), wills it to such an extent that he gave his life, will not cease to see to it that "for those who love God, all things work together unto good" (Rom. 8:28). In his own life and being he gives ample witness. Having suffered apparently complete failure and a most degrading death, he overcame and now enjoys the fullness of unending life in glory.

Regular *lectio* can keep us constantly in touch with the realities on which we can ground a solid hope. It also keeps us in touch with our solidarity with all our fellows and our call to love them with a self-giving love; it keeps us in touch with their solidarity with Christ, our God and our love: "Whatever you do to one of these the least of my brethren, you do to me" (Matt. 25:40). Oneness, identification with another, is the source of compassion—to be with another in that person's passion, feelings, sufferings, joys.

Through *meditatio* we will not only assimilate these truths so that they will inform our actions and mode of being but we will be enabled to share with others in an effective and powerful way a word of hope in the face of apocalypse. We will know in whom we believe (2 Tim. 1:12) and be able to bring him as Source of Life to others.

Such conviction leads to powerful and efficacious prayer (*oratio*). Saint James in the opening lines of his Letter tells us:

Let him ask God, who gives to all freely and ungrudgingly; it will be given him. But he must ask with faith, and no trace of doubt, because a person who has doubts is like the waves thrown up in the sea which the wind drives. That sort of person, in two minds, wavering between going different ways, must not expect that the Lord will give him anything. (James 1:5–8)

We all pay lip service to the importance and power of prayer. But does our practice belie our words? Are we really in touch with the power we have through prayer?

When we make something, say a table, we take some wood or some other material that is at hand, shape it and put it together, set the table on its four legs, and walk away. It can go on very well without us, for we used pre-existing materials that do not need us to keep existing. The shape we have given them abides in them. But when God makes something he does not use pre-existing materials. It may not be wholly accurate to say he makes them out of nothing. In fact, he shares with them something of his own being and goodness. "One is good—God" (Mark 10:18). If he steps back from his creation it simply ceases to exist. In his sharing, at every moment he is bringing it forth. And he has willed that the way in which he is going to bring forth this creation today, tomorrow, and the next day can be determined in part by our prayer: "Ask and you shall receive" (Matt. 7:7). This is the power of our prayer. It harnesses the creative energy of God. We can by our prayer, if we waver not in our hearts, make a great difference in the way this world works for everyone. It is undoubtedly the prayer of some of the just that at this very moment holds back the consummation of the threat of nuclear annihilation. Let us pray.

It is contemplation (*contemplatio*) that leads us most powerfully into compassion. It is true that, because of the solidarity of the human race and the more profound oneness of the baptized in Christ, whenever any one of us rises through contemplation to new levels of consciousness the whole human family is raised. Any bit of leaven will leaven the entire mass.

We certainly do need a transformation of consciousness. Never has it been known in the history of tribes or nations that a people have stockpiled weapons and not in the end used them. But if we use the weapons we have stockpiled it will mark the end of a civilization. We definitely need to change our human pattern and rise to a new level of consciousness that will enable us to pound our weapons into plowshares and feed the hungry of the earth.

As each one of us enters into the deeper places through contemplation, we come to see ourselves in our truest being, at the Source of our being in God. We come to see ourselves each moment coming forth from our Source, and not only ourselves but all others with us. By the intuition of the Spirit we come to know our solidarity with all being. This cannot but lead to compassion—compassion for our fellow humans who are one with us in our Source, in our call, and in our fate. We will know that in their completeness lies our completeness, and vice versa. We will continue to seek our own fullness, that we might be a source of fullness. And we will suffer our fellows' lack and rejoice in their fullness as our own lack and fullness. Moreover, we will know that oneness and compassion with the rest of creation that is the source of good stewardship and a true ecology.

Contemplation does not lead to inactivity. It is in itself the highest actuality of our being. In its compassion it leads to the deepest concern and the fullest activity, according to our particular vocations, for the well-being of the entire human family and its global environment. One cannot steadily see the created reality in the face of the loving and compassionate Father and not be transformed and transforming.

In the face of apocalypse anything less is not sufficient. And yet in the face of the horrendous vastness of apocalypse or its particular expression in nuclear holocaust, ten minutes of *lectio* a day seems like a most insignificant resource. It is small enough that it is readily available to absolutely everyone. Yet it contains the mustard seed of the Gospel. If it is firmly planted in one's life and allowed to mature it can indeed shelter the whole of creation.

We all want our lives to make a difference. Some things can only be known by experience. Those who are unwilling to risk experience will never know. They can be helped along by the witness of Christians who do obviously see and give a living witness of the fruits of the Spirit, love, joy, and peace, even in the midst of effective compassion and identification with the victims of deterrence, despoliation, and social oppression.

Lectio is a very simple source, a simplicity that opens the gates of heaven itself. It is simple yet powerful, for it harnesses all the goodness, power, love, and mercy of God himself. Is there anything more? Is there anything else?

> I am listening. What is Yahweh saying?
> *What God is saying means peace*
> for his people, for his friends,
> if only they renounce their folly;
> for those who fear him, his saving help is near,
> and the glory will then live in our country.
>
> (Ps. 85:8–9)

III. THEOLOGICAL RESOURCES

5. Liberating the Divine Energy

ROSEMARY HAUGHTON

We need to discover a way to make real in the world of conscious vision and decision what the words in the title of this book reveal. How can we really make society compassionate? How do we uncover interdependence, reveal the necessity of cooperation for human—that is, spiritual—survival? What are our *resources* for all that? The word *resource* itself indicates a means of supplying a want, or a stock that can be drawn upon. But it is also an "expedient, device, *shift*," and it derives from the Latin *surgere*, "to rise." Rise? Shift? Is there a need for some kind of imaginative leap, an embracing view from a different vantage point beyond our present range—a paradigmatic shift? Is this the resource we need—a different kind of consciousness?

There is a comic quality about the answer to this, because it seems naive to atheists and theologians alike; it has something of the crude humor of the top-hatted gentleman slipping on the banana skin, thus assuming with reluctant and speedy humility a viewpoint unfamiliar to him but well known to very small children. Yet, to appreciate it (if he were willing to do so), he would need an artist's imagination and a philosopher's patient curiosity. For what Christians need to suggest is that one man did have the resources, feel the compassion, breathe the spirit, recognize the social reality, and reveal the reality bonding all these things; and that he said it and lived it, and was half heard and less than half obeyed; but that something got through and was picked up by a succession of strange women and men, who were sometimes acclaimed (generally for the wrong reasons) but often ignored, misunderstood, mocked, or illtreated (or even killed), and occasionally canonized later.

The resources for social compassion (spiritual, that is, *real* ones) are available to us and have been from our cradles, though we have so far lost the vision of childhood that we also need a great deal of help in recovering a point of view that will enable us to interpret them, and I shall suggest that the disturbing explorations of modern physics may serve as our Western banana skin. We also need the wisdom of Eastern teachers who have seen things buried by us under layers of reductionist, greedy pseudoreason but that lead us back to the Christian foundations and ask us to look again, with a simplicity bordering on the foolish, at the things the Gospels say. "Matthew, Mark, Luke, and John, bless the bed that I lie on," and bless us with insight to catch a little of what you only partly understood and yet labored so honestly and courageously to communicate.

We need a different kind of Gospel commentary, less like a dictionary and more like a play, for we have to come to this work with imagination above all. There has been, and must be, careful analysis and comparison. We need all that patient (and imaginative) scholarship has been able to reveal, because without it imagination has breath but no wings; it soars on the spirit with pinions whose bones are meticulous historical and linguistic inquiry. But it is only by means of informed and intelligent imagination that we may be able to enter into the vision of human potential that Jesus proclaimed so unambiguously. We need imagination to break through the accumulated theological presuppositions that come between us and the things Jesus did and said.

This is not to abdicate the role of intelligence, but to liberate it, in the way that it has been liberated many times by those who have made great leaps of creativity, leaps that come in moments of imaginative insight, characteristically described by such images as "a flash," "an explosion," "a revolution" of knowledge. It is only afterward that intelligence (which provided the raw materials) comes to grips with the new vision, plotting connections, drawing consequences, set free to explore and develop a previously unimagined territory. It is in this way that we are beginning to realize, by a direct intuitive grasp, the amazing things that Jesus was aware of and lived by and wanted to share.

This sounds almost as if none before us had got the point, and the vast wealth of Christian mystical and social-visionary writing prove the contrary, as do the lives of the many who lived it out with passion and wisdom. But there is a sense in which it has required the degree of hindsight we have by virtue of the passage of time, as well as the understanding of the processes of cultural and political development, to bring us to the point where we can perceive some important things. The role of politics in the development of dogma is one of them; we can understand also the shaping power of cultural expectations, of fully internalized and therefore unacknowledged value systems, and of equally unquestioned cultural assumptions about the nature of reality (and of "nature") in modifying or even denying the direction taken by the movement initiated by Jesus. We do not and cannot deny two thousand years of struggle and hope, but we can acknowledge with gratitude the potential for a paradigmatic shift in our awareness of the message Jesus proclaimed and was, and the promise this holds for our world, if we are able to accept it.

In understanding better what Jesus was doing and thinking, it is helpful to compare him with John the Baptist. The followers of Jesus saw John as the forerunner and were careful to emphasize his subsidiary function, but to Jesus himself John was an inspiration, a catalyst, a model, whom at first he imitated in many ways. It is interesting therefore to see how and why that changed. John's approach was prophetic within a certain clear prophetic tradition. He foresaw the coming of disaster, and he had every practical reason for doing so, in the unstable and explosive situation of the day. His interpretation of what he saw was traditional—if you repent, if the people of God turn once more to justice and purity of heart, the doom will not fall except on the ungodly. His message was a call to restore the time of just relationships affirmed by Moses and violated by greedy and power-seeking religious professionals. The change he called for benefited the poor and weak, but it was to be a restoration, by however drastic methods. The chaff was to be winnowed out so that the good grain might be used to feed the people, yet it was an old and well-tried recipe.

At first this was the message of Jesus also. He came out of the same strand of Jewish spirituality and may well have discussed with his cousin the meaning of the times, for it seems that his own interpretation and proposed remedy were similar: Doom is very near, it is the fruit of greed and oppression and deceit. But something else is imminent if only people can see it—there is an alternative. He called it the Kingdom, or reign, of God. John's vision, though apocalyptic in the popular sense, did not reveal or uncover anything new. He called for a recovery of the golden age of simplicity and justice, and to this also Jesus called those who heard him, but Jesus soon found himself discovering more than John's doctrine seemed to envisage.

One key was Jesus' sensitivity to actual individual people, in whom he perceived the operation of the same divine energy that was his own motive power. He knew them not only as acted upon by divine power but as sources of it. This was the fruit of his compassion; he "suffered with" those whom he met and who sought him out, and there was an intimate exchange of feeling and understanding in which the distinctions between persons seemed hard to define. When he said to the paralytic, or the blind man or the shamed woman, "*Your faith* has saved you— healed you," he was acknowledging the power of a transaction, a flowing of knowledge and power between them, in which his compassion was an essential agent yet one that was powerless without the response that somehow completed the circuit and transformed the situation.

We are aware of this in the words, the decisive, distinctive sayings that have come through to us, uniquely his beyond all editorial adaptation or modification. "Blessed are you poor . . ." who are aware of need, open to change, not closed off by the need to cling to what you have, for the divine energy can flow in you, transform, heal, liberate. "No one puts new wine in old wineskins," however strong they look; it simply doesn't work. Jesus saw it not working, for the still fermenting wine of genuine compassion was apocalyptic; it revealed a newness that split the old containers wide open, and the guardians of those containers were outraged. John had frightened and offended them by challenging their stewardship, but he did it on familiar ground. Jesus uttered the same challenge, but instead of giving them the option of exercising more justly the roles they filled, he seemed to be saying—and demonstrating—that they no longer had a role in any sense they could understand or accept.

It was a gradual process, as all discovery must be, however revolutionary. He felt that the law was indeed holy, that the teachers were to be obeyed, and he was himself an observant, religious person—or at least he set out to be one. But he found it less and less possible to reconcile the power of compassion he was experiencing with the institutional attempts to interpret the righteousness of God. So he found himself, almost without intending it, breaking categories and ignoring hallowed divisions, and thus beginning to create an alternative social order.

Most of his followers found this impossible to understand. To the end they struggled somehow to fit his behavior and words into the framework of expectations familiar to them, those, indeed, with which he himself had been raised, if Luke's evocation of Mary's theology in the Magnificat is anything to go by. They expected a reversal of power, a reign of justice in which the poor would triumph, as indeed most revolutionary movements have done. They also hoped that the religious establishment, or at least a significant part of it, would recognize the leadership of Jesus as in line with prophecy and official messianic doctrine, and they were increasingly upset when this didn't happen.

It is not surprising that for us the problem of interpretation is quite severe. The only documents we have were composed by people who, while striving to be faithful to the message that had transformed them, could not help interpreting it more or less in terms of the only cultural and religious models they had. Yet it is possible, and increasingly urgent, to use these resources in order to perceive more clearly what Jesus perceived and proposed.

One way in which we can assist that perception is by recognizing that the process of discovery that we can observe in the experience of Jesus is essentially the same one that has been pursued by prophets, visionaries, and revolutionaries within the tradition that stems from him. As with Jesus himself, the discovery is a theological one, but it emerges as a result of personal and often painful experiences, in which direct and self-validating awareness of what God is calling forth in human beings in particular situations—the potential for transformation in God's image—is blocked and denied by the structures created in the name of God. This experience forces a re-expression of what God is like and, therefore, of how human beings are to be encountered.

Jesus found himself able to liberate the divine energy in people, and over and over again this produced a psychophysical transformation that came neither from him nor from the other person, taken in isolation, but was the fruit of their encounter. It happened *between* them. "Faith" was that act of opening that made possible this reciprocal dynamic, and although he seems to have tried to contain the phenomenon within the traditional structures of his religion, it could not be done. The new experience of God demanded a new social organism, a different model of reality. And this has been the experience through the centuries of those who have somehow recaptured the vision that Jesus lived and empowered. Try as they would to fit in, they found themselves in conflict with those claiming to represent and make available the divine energy.

Sometimes their sheer holiness impressed the religious authorities so much that they actually shifted a little to make a space for the new vision, inevitably cramping it in the process and making it one option among others, a freakish alternative for the few rather than a way to freedom for anyone (this is what happened to Francis of Assisi). Sometimes prophets are tamed by their own loyalties, and women have been especially vulnerable to the kind of moral bullying that makes people doubt their own vision. Sometimes they have been driven out, or departed, to try to recreate the gospel reality in the wilderness, like George Fox and Margaret Fell. Sometimes they were suppressed, or killed, like Jesus himself.

In our time, the time of apocalypse, the realization of what Jesus discovered is less possible to evade. The significance of his unwanted but inescapable conflict with the religious establishment is unavoidable in the light of our historical perspective. The kinds of language and analysis that have enabled us to see his struggle in political, and at the same time spiritual, terms make it much easier for us to perceive the social imperative of compassion, though certainly not easier to embody it in choices and decisions.

The central theological axis of all this seems to be the experience of Jesus that compassion both requires and creates: a certain kind of social relatedness, in fact, a society. Moreover, this society and the compassion that is its energy are the mode and locus of God's presence with humankind. Jesus' own image for this—the Kingdom, or reign, of God—was not original, and today it causes problems for many people because it has hierarchical, authoritarian, and oppressive connotations and for women, especially, recalls themes of male domination. This is inevitable, because the intervening models of kingship have all been based on static pyramidal images of dominance and unquestioned, arbitrary authority.

These are good reasons for finding other images, but it is still important to realize that *kingdom* or *reign*, as Jesus used the term, is not at all an image of dominance or static hierarchy. It is, rather, drawing on the vision of the Old Testament prophets, an image of variety and harmony, a network of mutually supportive relationships (even between individuals normally regarded as antipathetic, such as lions and lambs!), a society in which work is productive and satisfying, a spirit of joy and celebration is prominent, and a sense of health and personal dignity and wholeness are basic. It is a dynamic vision, depending on the unchecked flow of trust and caring between individuals, that creates from the interaction of many a greater and satisfying whole, of which the "king"—the animator and in a sense the being—is God alone, whose name is compassion, whose nature is an inflowing and outflowing of life.

It is therefore clearly a political vision, but an anarchistic one as far as human authority is concerned. The Kingdom of God, or of Heaven, is a dynamic image whose political "shape" depends on the absence of artificial barriers to the flow of divine energy. This is why compassion is the key to the whole situation now, as it was for Jesus—the violent and inescapable experience of finding oneself involved with another's suffering, or joy. When Jesus "had compassion" on people, whether individuals or multitudes, he found himself driven, even against his desire or common sense, to allow the flow of the encounter to lead to its appropriate results. So he found himself sharing table fellowship with racketeers, talking intimately with women, embracing the diseased, making friends with pagans, and driving himself to the point of nervous exhaustion in his reluctance to repulse the sick and wretched who thronged around him.

In all this he walked through every kind of social and religious barrier, smashing categories as the child smashes the ice on puddles. But although the exhilaration, the sense of joy and freedom, that resulted is manifest in his own reactions as well as in those of his new and peculiar friends, he did not break conventions out of defiance or to attract attention, though he knew well how to make a public, symbolic point when he felt it was necessary. He was even rather reluctant to break with convention, and he himself needed to be challenged to see the implications of abiding by them, as in the story of the Syro-Phoenician woman. He broke categories because he couldn't help it, and if we are looking for "proofs" of his "divinity," we might do worse than notice the God-like quality of a man whose very nature seemed impossible to confine within even the most sacred religious expectations. There was something in him stronger even than his own explicit theology at any given moment; his theological understanding was constantly in process of being split open by the power of the compassion of God.

We have, then, a resource for social compassion, which is in fact a demand for a compassionate society. It is the divine energy as we perceive it at work in Jesus of Nazareth and as we thereby know it to be the essential reality of ourselves. But in order to help us to embody that reality we need the power of a liberated imagination; we need images and models more adequate to our experience than the plate-armor of Greek-derived, dualistic, and static language within which Christian theology has had to stifle for so long. (The amazing thing is that so much dynamic vision and living has managed to break through all that in every century, and even somehow to give life to inadequate concepts themselves, at least for a time.)

The language of a different concept of reality can liberate Christianity to grow from its roots with amazing vigor. What is happening now in the churches is a new growth, which has bred a new language but has also been bred by it, in that paradoxical and yet clearly observable way, blurring cause and effect, that can itself only be expressed by a language radically different from Aristotelian and Cartesian categories. Some of its concepts derive from, or have been influenced by, those whose studies and experience have driven them to work and imagine on the frontiers of the conceivable, whether in subatomic physics or in the regions of the mind. The strangest thing for many has been the convergence of thought in these two areas. It is the discoveries of the physicists that have especially excited amazement, hostility, and a huge sense of possibility. Their unsettling explorations are indeed apocalyptic, revealing an experience of acausal dynamic relationships that cannot in any way be described with reference to the models of reality the West (whether secular or religious) has inherited from the Enlightenment.

Many people who are not particularly religious have become aware (sometimes with mixed feelings) that scientists have begun to talk a language verging on the mystical. Some scientists are excited about it, others disgusted and struggling, and the religious world is often not too happy with a way of talking that seems to blur the distinction between natural and supernatural. That is, of course, precisely what it does. It is also what Jesus did, to the alarm of many religious people who knew exactly what that implied of threat to their system.

Consider a definition, by Henry Shapp of the University of California, of elementary particles: an elementary particle is not, he says, "an independently existing and analyzable entity. It is, in essence, *a set of relationships* that *reach outwards* to other things," which sounds very much like a theological or even a romantic statement. A long time ago, James Jeans already felt that "the stream of knowledge is heading towards a non-mechanical reality; the universe begins to look more like a great thought than a great machine." The conviction is now unavoidable among physicists that an "objective" description of phenomena is not possible, because the observer not only is part of the process but actually changes the answers by the kinds of questions that are asked. The universe is discovered to be an interconnected web of dynamic relations, events rather than objects, and it is perceived that consciousness itself may well be an essential aspect of the universe.

Then, too, reality is seen as a series of what Koestler called "holons," which are both wholes and parts—parts of a greater system that is itself part of a still greater, and so on, and a whole that has parts that are wholes also, integrating further parts. But these wholes and parts are living, they are organisms that develop, change, transmute; and the strange thought emerges from various respectable scientists that the earth is itself a being, a living organism of many integrated parts and once (and now again) expressed under the name of Gaea, goddess of earth. But "mind is the essence of being alive," as Fritz Capra puts it in *The Turning Point,* and the earth's being is an organism that lives, in the countless interrelations, the exchanges of life, that sustain her subsystems.

Beyond all this, yet not beyond, is a thought, a mind that is somehow the "self-organizing dynamic of the entire cosmos," to quote from Capra again. Father, Mother, the life that integrates and frees, the organizing principle of "the Kingdom of heaven": This God is intimately present in all things, yet is other, strange, beyond conception or description. This God is neither natural nor supernatural but is experienced with and beyond all phenomena, is manifested in transcendent experience but only so as to be the more recognizable in the ordinary ones to which human beings have somehow restricted their world. And in the increasing number of areas to which the new perceptions extend (mystical, psychological, scientific) we begin to realize the wholeness to which human beings are called, a harmony within each person that grows from, and enables, a harmony between people and between people and other creatures: a physical, social, ecological, spiritual harmony becomes conceivable.

It becomes clear that those powers that we have regarded as unusual, available to the especially gifted or the especially holy—healing, second sight, independence of the "laws" of human metabolism or of gravity, even the oddities of bilocation—are powers proper to all human beings and capable of being developed in ways and degrees that have hitherto been explored mainly by writers of science fiction. It is not the mystics, saints, and seers who are abnormal, but the rest of us, ninety-nine percent blind, deaf, and ignorant.

Jesus was affirming and calling forth this power in those who trusted, who "had faith." His anger was enormous against those who confined men and women and denied them the fullness of life, for he knew what was possible. Compassion put him in touch with that and therefore fired both his enthusiasm and his anger.

We are beginning to realize that Jesus really did know what he was talking about in a more literal way than we have wanted to credit. There is dawning on us a new understanding of the way human beings are in the universe, drawing on the illuminating and Zen-like paradoxes of the physicists and the exploration of the inner world by Jung, Reich, and others. All this is giving us a different theological language, one of dynamic relations, one in which it is no longer ridiculous or "unscientific" to consider the power of compassion as a key factor in economics or medicine and in which the ultimate material of the universe is perceived to be love. The earth herself struggles to bring to birth a new humanity. The image is Paul's, but it is also the model that most accurately expresses the scientists' awareness of an inherently and dynamically related universe, a universe of love.

Through all this we are closely in touch with the thought and feeling of Jesus, and we are drawn to remember that early Christian writers turned to the Old Testament poetry of divine Wisdom when they were trying to find ways to express their sense of the otherness of Jesus, his transforming and transcendent being. Wisdom is always feminine, and she is brought vividly to consciousness as the poets of Wisdom, separated in time, unite to praise her. Her power is the divine power, she is the creative word of the Most High, she "made the circuit of the sky, traversed the depth of the abyss; the waves of the sea, the whole earth, every people and nation were under her sway" (Ecclus. 24:5–10). For she is "but one, yet can do every thing; herself unchanging she makes all things new, age after age she enters into holy souls and makes them friends of God and prophets" (Wisd. of Sol. 7:27).

This is mystical poetry, but it is also "science," and at the interchanges of mysticism and science, where the two flow into each other and are one stream, is the kind of awareness we have learned to call "right brain," the "feminine" kind of perception and thinking, which unifies and is aware of connections and movements. So it becomes apparent that the new language has to do with the emergence of that suppressed and despised kind of thinking associated with women, for lack of which our culture—and through it the whole earth—is in danger of death.

The women's movement has much to do with what is happening. It has released the possibility of taking seriously that life-giving potential that we had ignored and even hated, but it is itself fed by the emergence of new kinds of consciousness and learns to trust its own insights. The feminist consciousness is fast outgrowing its early temptation to identify with the masculine realm of left-brain, analytical, and mechanistic thinking in order to claim a place in the sun. The moon also has a lot to offer, and her ambiguous light reveals hidden things. The Christian feminist is struggling and praying and growing in this area, which is mapped by flowing patterns of paradox; she learns to balance limited but interconnected images of reality whose structural gaps are themselves essential parts of a new paradigm.

The focus is on relationship, the "between," in which beings are able to become themselves, as known to each other. And what brings the process into focus is in fact the act of compassion, which opens one to another in recognition of the "between-ness," of the exchanges that are the basis of being. Compassion cannot coexist with dominance, competition, or manipulation; it requires the encounter of friends, who are committed to knowing each other—not just knowing about each other. In the past, compassion was assigned to women because it was held to be a valuable social lubricant but not essential to the running of society and, on occasion, an intrusive nuisance that must be excluded from the theaters of power, as were women themselves. Now, women are beginning to assert what Jesus asserted, and was only half heard—that God's kind of society knows compassion not as an extra, or a "virtue" to be cultivated in one's spiritual backyard, but as the essential vital force that brings a society into being.

In practice, what kind of society? The new paradigms and the old Gospels agree: The society that permits the flowering of human potential is a society of friends in which there are neither masters nor servants. But friends have to know each other, and this limits the numbers, as Jesus limited the numbers. (Not to twelve, however, except for symbolic purposes; there were quite a few more than that, and many of them were women.) These groups of friends, therefore, must be communities or "churches," not isolated but exchanging life with one another, integrated and autonomous at their levels—"holons," knowing themselves as living parts of a greater whole.

Yet the greater whole is not an organization but an organism, "achieving a dynamic balance between self-assertive and integrative tendencies." All holons "act as interlaces and relay stations between systems levels" (Capra again), and so the local church and the "greater" thing called a church and the "lesser" thing called a person display an order whose nature is "not the transfer of power but the organization of complexity."

This is not a "churchy" matter for religious people in a religious realm apart from the world where real things are decided; this is Jesus' model, and the model revealed to us anew by adventurers on the frontiers of knowledge. It is a model of society as such, a world of humans and other beings whose relationship to one another at all levels is not concerned with "the transfer of control but the organization of complexity." At one level the model for all this is the *network*, in which the strength of the whole net depends on, but cannot control, the integrity of the knots, yet whose greatest area consists of holes!

As theological models these images are very close to the kind of society/church that Jesus passionately held to be possible. Of those to whom he proclaimed it, few then or later grasped the enormity of what he was asserting, as the rapid centralization and clericalization of the early church shows. They were not deliberately unfaithful; they could not grasp a paradigm so far, religiously and socially, from their expectations; and they can hardly be blamed, however tragic the results. It has taken the experience of two world wars and the threat of universal death, by nuclear weapons or just as horribly through the destruction of the earth's life-support systems, to force human beings to look for a different way of perceiving reality; and it required a scientific revolution far greater than that of Copernicus, Galileo, and Newton to supply the language for the perception that was so painfully clear to Jesus.

Divine Wisdom waits patiently for her children to open their eyes to what she offers, nurturing the tender shoots of understanding even in neglected places. Recent studies of the relationship of Jesus with women increasingly support the view that if anyone began dimly to understand the scope of what he was saying and doing it was the women disciples. This is not surprising, since they had nothing to gain from supporting the old patterns. The masculine vision of revolution might promise dominance for the previously dominated, but the women knew well that their own condition of subservience would continue even if that happened.

What Jesus offered was not a reversal of roles but their transformation, and somehow the women knew this. They lived it and clung to it and managed to carry it into the life of the community for a while. The New Testament documents themselves attest to the problems this created for the men who regarded themselves as the new churches' sole leaders and theologians. One does not make a big issue out of the leadership and speaking of women in the congregations if they are not very visibly leading and speaking. In the end the women lost the unequal battle. Their vision was never integrated into the official theology and discipline, and if any of them wrote, their writings were consigned to oblivion.

Yet the sense of their response, their experience, their living out of the Kingdom, is there to be recaptured. It is one of our most important resources, and it expresses itself naturally in the language of a compassionate, paradoxical reality. It is paradoxical because it is practical. It includes, it does not deny experiences but allows them; if their place in the pattern is not clear they are still allowed, so that a different image may emerge to affirm their value.

I am reminded of the scene in the movie *E.T.* in which the resurrected E.T., his heart pulsing visibly with renewed life and power, must be covered, zipped up, muffled, to save him from the power of an establishment that cannot deal with life but has a need to reduce life's oddness, its sweetness, its unpredictable energy, to a captive, analyzable and totally predictable *thing*—in fact, a dead one. That is a vivid image of what Christians have done with Jesus and, therefore, with that strangely powerful image of his that we call Eucharist.

Our resources for social compassion are right there—in the inescapable connectedness, the dynamic power, of the relation of friendship that explodes categories; the stimulation of inner (and outer) energies that simply make sin (sickness-despair-alienation) impossible; the feeding and being fed that is holiness, is social bonding, is the extreme "now" where past leads into future. We have effectively nullified all this; we have almost killed it. We have reduced Jesus to a source of moral guidelines but also to a source of moral blackmail similar to what was practiced by the religious establishment of his time. And we have made Eucharist a thing, a pill, or a community entertainment.

But the life is still there, the heart is pulsing. We need to get the live thing out of the wrappings and find out what it is really like when it is alive, yet we don't really want to. A church of friends, a world of compassion without domination or privilege, winners or losers—we dismiss that as impossible because our imaginations, conditioned by unexamined political and economic assumptions, cannot grasp it as a practical possibility. We are too accustomed to feeling that such a vision is either "utopian," meaning merely a speculation for idealists, or only possible as a minority exercise. And we are encouraged in this view by the many historical examples of attempts at it that have failed.

The reasons behind those failures bear examination. They turn out to have much to do with the eroding effects of sustained destructive criticism, or with unreal expectations, or—perhaps most importantly—with the Trojan horse of assumptions and expectations from the world of competition and dominance, brought in and welcomed by the unsuspecting pioneers. The fact that we are now able to know and assess this makes a difference, though the dangers are still there.

Another reason that we dismiss the possibility of Jesus' kind of world is that we are afraid of it. In all honesty we have to admit that if such a transformation were to take place we stand to lose a great deal. It takes a great deal of compassion, more than most of us have, to allow such an uncovering.

That is why the vision of Jesus is necessarily social; it cannot be envisaged or borne by individuals. The new paradigm of resurrection can only be allowed to emerge if people begin (however timidly) to sense the flow of life between them, a giving and receiving of compassion socially that can gradually enlarge the channels of communicated being. In the end we may realize that our fears are unreal and imposed; our only reality is that life that knows no categories or limits.

IV. HISTORICAL RESOURCES

6. Impasse and Dark Night

CONSTANCE FITZGERALD, O.C.D.

A number of issues in contemporary Christian spirituality under-
pin and influence the theological interpretation developed in
this chapter. Today our spirituality is rooted in experience and
in story: the experience and story of women (poor women, black
women, white women, exploited women, Asian women, Native
American women, etc.); the experience of the poor and oppressed of the world; the experience of the aging; the experience of the fear of nuclear holocaust and the far-reaching evils
of nuclear buildup for the sake of national security, power, and
domination; the experience of the woundedness of the earth and
the environment.

This experience is nourished with meaning by history. It values, therefore, the interpretation of and dialogue with classical
sources, with the story of the tradition. Within this framework,
Christian spirituality remains attentive to the centrality of the
self—to stages of faith development, to passages, to crises of
growth—in one's search for God and human wholeness. It
reaches, moreover, with particular urgency in our own time for
the integration of contemplation and social commitment.

Against this background, I hope to interpret John of the
Cross' concept and symbolism of "dark night" (including his
classical signs concerning the passage from meditation to contemplation) to show what new understanding it brings to the
contemporary experience of what I would call impasse, which
insinuates itself inescapably and uninvited into one's inner life
and growth and into one's relationships.[1] What is even more
significant today is that many of our *societal* experiences open
into profound impasse, for which we are not educated, particularly as Americans.

This brings me to two assumptions. First, our experience of

God and our spirituality must emerge from our concrete, historical situation and must return to that situation to feed it and enliven it. Second, I find a great number of dark night or impasse experiences, personal and societal, that cry out for meaning. There is not only the so-called dark night of the soul but the dark night of the world. What if, by chance, our time in evolution is a dark-night time—a time of crisis and transition that must be understood if it is to be part of learning a new vision and harmony for the human species and the planet?

To discover meaning, there is value in bringing contemporary impasse into dialogue with the classical text of John.[2] In unfolding the mystery of dark night and unpacking its symbolism in response to the experience of impasse, I would hope to help others understand, name, and claim this experience of God and thereby direct their own creative and affective energy.

IMPASSE

By impasse, I mean that there is no way out of, no way around, no rational escape from, what imprisons one, no possibilities in the situation. In a true impasse, every normal manner of acting is brought to a standstill, and ironically, impasse is experienced not only in the problem itself but also in any solution rationally attempted. Every logical solution remains unsatisfying, at the very least. The whole life situation suffers a depletion, has the word *limits* written upon it. Dorothée Soelle describes it as "unavoidable suffering," an apt symbol of which is physical imprisonment, with its experience of being squeezed into a confined space. Any movement out, any next step, is canceled, and the most dangerous temptation is to give up, to quit, to surrender to cynicism and despair, in the face of the disappointment, disenchantment, hopelessness, and loss of meaning that encompass one.

It is not difficult to imagine how such attitudes affect self-image and sense of worth and turn back on the person or group to engender a sense of failure, to reinforce a realization—not always exact—that their own mistakes have contributed to the ambiguity.

Moreover, intrinsic to the experience of impasse is the impression and feeling of rejection and lack of assurance from those on whom one counts. At the deepest levels of impasse, one sees the support systems on which one has depended pulled out from under one and asks if anything, if anyone, is trustworthy. Powerlessness overtakes the person or group caught in impasse and opens into the awareness that no understandable defense is possible. This is how impasse looks to those who are imprisoned within it. It is the experience of disintegration, of deprivation of worth, and it has many faces, personal and societal.

There is, however, another dimension of impasse that philosophers and psychologists, sociologists and theologians, poets and mystics, have reflected upon from their particular perspectives. Belden Lane, director of historical theology at Saint Louis University, indicates it in his article, *Spirituality and Political Commitment:*

. . . in a genuine impasse one's accustomed way of acting and living is brought to a standstill. The left side of the brain, with its usual application of linear, analytical, conventional thinking is ground to a halt. The impasse forces us to start all over again, driving us to contemplation. On the other hand, the impasse provides a challenge and a concrete focus for contemplation. . . . It forces the right side of the brain into gear, seeking intuitive, symbolic, unconventional answers, so that action can be renewed eventually with greater purpose.[3]

The negative situation constitutes a reverse pressure on imagination so that imagination is the only way to move more deeply into the experience. It is this "imaginative shock," or striking awareness that our categories do not fit our experience, that throws the intuitive, unconscious self into gear in quest of what the possibilities really are.

Paradoxically, a situation of no potential is loaded with potential, and impasse becomes the place for the reconstitution of the intuitive self. This means the situation of being helpless can be efficacious, not merely self-denying and demanding of passivity. While nothing seems to be moving forward, one is, in fact, on a homeward exile—*if* one can yield in the right way, responding with *full consciousness* of one's suffering in the impasse yet daring to believe that new possibilities, beyond immediate vision, can be given.

It must be stressed, writes Dorothée Soelle, that insofar as the experience of impasse, or suffering, is repressed, "there is a corresponding disappearance of passion for life and of the strength and intensity of its joys" and insights.[4] The person caught in impasse must find a way to identify, face, live with, and express this suffering. If one cannot speak about one's affliction in anguish, anger, pain, lament—at least to the God within—one will be destroyed by it or swallowed up by apathy. Every attempt to humanize impasse must begin with this phenomenon of experienced, acknowledged powerlessness, which can then activate creative forces that enable one to overcome the feeling that one is without power.[5]

A genuine impasse situation is such that the more action one applies to escape it, the worse it gets. The principles of "first order change"—reason, logic, analysis, planning—do not work, as studies by three Stanford psychiatrists try to show. Thoroughgoing impasse forces one, therefore, to end one's habitual methods of acting by a radical breaking out of the conceptual blocks that normally limit one's thinking.

Genuine change occurs through a "second order" response, "one which rethinks the solution previously tried and suggests something altogether unexpected. The quality of paradox is at the heart of 'second order change.' "[6] It implies that the unexpected, the alternative, the new vision, is not given on demand but is beyond conscious, rational control. It is the fruit of unconscious processes in which the situation of impasse itself becomes the focus of contemplative reflection.[7]

The psychologists and the theologians, the poets and the mystics, assure us that impasse can be the condition for creative growth and transformation *if* the experience of impasse is fully appropriated within one's heart and flesh with consciousness and consent; *if* the limitations of one's humanity and human condition are squarely faced and the sorrow of finitude allowed to invade the human spirit with real, existential powerlessness; *if* the ego does not demand understanding in the name of control and predictability but is willing to admit the mystery of its own being and surrender itself to this mystery; *if* the path into the unknown, into the uncontrolled and unpredictable margins of life, is freely taken when the path of deadly clarity fades.

DARK NIGHT IN JOHN OF THE CROSS

When I am able to situate a person's experience of impasse within the interpretive framework of dark night, that person is reassured and energized to live, even though she feels she is dying. The impasse is opened to meaning precisely because it can be redescribed.

In order to understand dark night, it is important to realize that John of the Cross begins and ends with love and desire in his poems and prose writings.[8] He is intent on showing what kind of affective education is carried on by the Holy Spirit over a lifetime. He delineates, therefore, the movement from a desire, or love, that is possessive, entangled, complex, selfish, and unfree to a desire that is fulfilled with union with Jesus Christ and others. In the process of affective redemption, desire is not suppressed or destroyed but gradually transferred, purified, transformed, set on fire. We go *through* the struggles and ambiguities of human desire to integration and personal wholeness.

This means there is a dark side to human desire, and the experience of dark night is the way that desire is purified and freed.[9] What is important to realize is that it is *in* the very experience of darkness and joylessness, in the suffering and withdrawal of accustomed pleasure, that this transformation is taking place. Transfiguration does not happen at the end of the road; it is in the making now. If we could see the underside of this death, we would realize it is already resurrection. Since we are not educated for darkness, however, we see this experience, because of the shape it takes, as a sign of *death.* Dark night is instead a sign of *life,* of growth, of development in our relationship with God, in our best human relationships, and in our societal life. It is a sign to move on in hope to a new vision, a new experience.

Night in John of the Cross, which symbolically moves from twilight to midnight to dawn, is the progressive purification and transformation of the human person *through* what we cherish or desire and through what give us security and support.[10] We are affected by darkness, therefore, where we are mostly deeply involved and committed, and in what we love and care for most. Love makes us vulnerable, and it is love itself and its development that precipitate darkness in oneself and in the "other."

Only when love has grown to a certain point of depth and commitment can its limitations be experienced. Our senses are carried to deeper perception, as it were, by exhaustion. A fullness in one way of being and relating makes one touch its limits. This is not a question of disgust, as it often appears and feels like, but of a movement through sensual pleasure and joy to deeper, stronger faithfulness and to the experience of a love and a commitment, a hope and a vision, unimagined and unexpected on this side of darkness.

We all need some satisfaction of our desire in order to begin and go on in prayer, relationship, or ministry, but it is the withdrawal of pleasure and the confrontation with limitation (our own and others') that signals the transition or growth crisis of the dark night. The test is whether we can, in the last analysis, maintain the direction or momentum of our life without either glancing off permanently into another direction to escape, or succumbing to the darkness of total despair.[11]

Love (romance!) makes us hunger for the unambivalent situation. Yet it is in the very light of love that we encounter the opaqueness of our own humanness and experience the destructiveness within ourselves and the "other." Ambiguity arises, on the one hand, from human inadequacy; it arises, on the other hand, from the Spirit of God calling us beyond ourselves, beyond where we are, into transcendence. We are being challenged to make the passage from loving, serving, "being with," because of the pleasure and joy it gives us, to loving and serving regardless of the cost. We are being challenged to a reacceptance of the "other."[12]

Every God relationship, every significant human love, every marriage, every ministry, every relationship between a person and a community, and perhaps every human group and every nation will come to this point of impasse, with its intrinsic demands for and promise of a new vision, a new experience of God, a quieter, deeper, freer, more committed love. And it will come precisely when imagination seems paralyzed, when intimacy seems eroded, and when desire feels dead.

This brings us to John of the Cross' signs for discerning the genuineness of the dark night purification. Traditionally, they have been recognized as theological signs of the passage in prayer from discursive meditation to contemplation and are, therefore, descriptive of one's spiritual development, one's intrapersonal life. A careful reading of John of the Cross, integrated with concrete human experience, would seem to indicate, however, that the interpretation of these signs must be extended to one's interpersonal life as well, and perhaps even to one's societal life. I submit that a societal interpretation of these signs, and dark night in general, throws considerable light on the contemporary experience of societal impasse.

Although John seems to delineate a smooth transition, his developmental model includes breakdown and failure. This is why the signs speak to us of death, even though they are in reality signs of development and growth. There are two sets of signs, one in the second book of the *Ascent of Mount Carmel* (chap. 13, nos. 2–4); the other in the first book of the *Dark Night* (chap. 9, nos. 2–8). Although the perspective is different in each (the *Ascent* signs are given from the side of the person's faith response, the *Dark Night* signs from God's side), the signs are the same and can be correlated.

The first set of signs underlines one's powerlessness to pray with one's reason or rational mind "since God does not communicate himself through the senses as he did before, by means of the discursive analysis and synthesis of ideas, but begins to communicate himself through pure spirit by an act of simple contemplation in which there is no discursive succession of thought." The senses cannot attain to this contemplation, and dryness results.[13]

Basic to the experience of disintegration or dark night is an apparent breakdown of communication and a powerlessness to do anything about it. One's usual way of functioning, or relating, provides no satisfaction and does not work. What formerly was essential for growth and fidelity (e.g., an active choice and decision for Christ in reasoned meditation) now hinders growth.[14] Nothing happens in meditation. One cannot relate to the loved one as before. The system on which one depends breaks down. Certainty and pleasure give way to ambiguity, misunderstanding, and dryness or boredom.

It is difficult to realize, except by hindsight, that a new kind of love and deeper level of communication, transcending the former love, is developing and is already operative (contemplation). Accustomed to receiving love and insight in one way, one perceives this communication and situation as darkness. What is, in fact, a call to a new vision and to deeper, more genuine intimacy with God, with the "other," and with the world, is experienced as less commitment and less love, precisely because the call comes when intimacy seems to be falling apart and limitation looms large. There seems no possibility of movement backward or forward but only imprisonment, lack of vision, and failure of imagination. "Everything seems to be functioning in reverse," writes John, in this forced passage from rational, analytical, linear thinking to intuitive, metaphorical, symbolic consciousness.[15]

In his probing article "Atheism and Contemplation," Michael J. Buckley shows that John of the Cross, like Feuerbach, is very "sensitive to the humanization consciousness works on its God." John is acutely aware, with Freud, that the religious movement toward God can emerge either from the desire for satisfaction or from the drive for reassurance.[16] In other words, John is conscious of the tendency of religion to become projection and is always subtly asking the question What is the focus of your desire, of your religious awareness and its commitment? "He takes the theological dictum, 'Whatever is received is received according to the mode of the one receiving it,' and he applies it to a person's conceptions and images of God."[17]

Because in the initial stages of the spiritual life, and even in the more advanced ones, the sensory part of the soul is imperfect, it frequently receives God's spirit with this very imperfection.[18]

We make our God, or gods, in our own image. "Our understanding and our loves are limited by what we are. What we grasp and what we long for is very much shaped and determined by our own nature and personality-set," writes Buckley. If this is not changed by the Spirit of Jesus gradually permeating individual experiences and influencing patterns of development and growth, "there is no possibility of [the] contemplation of anything but our own projections."[19] John of the Cross is at pains to show how our images of God are progressively and of necessity changed and shattered by life experience. The very experience of dark night does, in fact, critique our present images of God. As Buckley says,

The continual contemplative purification of the human person is a progressive hermeneutic of the nature of God. The self-disclosure of God . . . is finally only possible within the experience of the contradiction of finite concepts and human expectations. The darkness and its pain are here, but they are finely dialectical movements in which the human is purified from projection by a "no" which is most radically a "yes." The disclosures of God contradict the programs and expectations of human beings in order to fulfill human desire and human freedom at a much deeper level than subjectivity would have measured out its projections.[20]

When, in the first sign, we reflect on the breakdown of communication and relationship, therefore, we are assuming also a change and a shattering of one's images. This causes confusion and a sense of loss and meaninglessness.

This is not a defense of Christian masochism, as Dorothée Soelle calls it, nor a sadistic understanding of God, but rather a recognition of the ongoing process of self-acceptance and reacceptance of the "other" that is necessary for real, enduring love and progressive, mutual insight and creativity. This process presupposes that, in every significant relationship, we come to the experience of limitation, our own and others'. We come to the point where we must withdraw and reclaim our projections of God, of friend, of ministry, of community, and let the "others" be who and what they are: mystery.

The emphasis in the second set of signs is on emptiness in life experience and deadness of desire. Not only is prayer dry, but life is dry, relationship is dry, ministry is dry.

Souls do not get satisfaction or consolation from the things of God [and] they do not get any out of creatures either. Since God puts a soul in this dark night in order to dry up and purge its sensory appetite, he does not allow it to find sweetness or delight in anything.[21]

John assures us the time must come in our development when neither God, nor the "other," nor one's life project satisfy, but only disappoint, disillusion, and shatter one's naive hope.

Because desire seems dead, because there is no inclination to do anything about the situation, because one really ceases to care, the temptation to quit, to walk away, becomes overpowering. Hopelessness and worthlessness invade one's perception and one's psyche. It is in the throes of this crisis that people abandon God and prayer, a marriage, a friend, a ministry, a community, a church, and forfeit forever the new vision, the genuine hope, the maturity of love and loyalty, dedication and mutuality, that is on the other side of darkness and hopelessness. Darkness is the place where egoism dies and true unselfish love for the "other" is set free. Moreover, it is the birthplace of a vision and a hope that cannot be imagined this side of darkness.

John can write about self-knowledge as a primary effect of the dark night for two reasons. First, the light and development of contemplative love show up one's limitations. Second, the withdrawal of accustomed pleasure in life, and the consequent frustration of desire, trigger one's seemingly destructive tendencies and move them into action on a level that is beyond conscious control.[22]

What must be remembered at all costs is that desire is not destroyed. Rather, right in this situation of unassuaged emptiness and apparent deadness of desire, in the very area of life in which one is most involved and therefore most vulnerable, desire is being purified, transformed, and carried into deeper, more integrated passion. Dark night mediates the transfiguration of affectivity, and obstacles conceal within themselves untold, hidden energy.

Here we sense what powerful symbolism dark night is. It is an image of productivity and speaks of life buried in its opposite: life concealed, life invisible, life unseen in death.

Thus the third set of signs has two different moments, moving from painful anxiety about culpability to a new and deeper level of appreciation of God and/or the "other" in a quiet, loving attentiveness. John describes the suffering side of this experience when he writes,

The memory ordinarily turns to God solicitously and with painful care, and the soul thinks it is not serving God but turning back, because it is aware of this distaste for the things of God.[23]

Here it is a question of being obsessed with the problem. How much easier it would be to bear the darkness were one not conscious of one's failures and mistakes. The most confusing and damnable part of the dark night is the suspicion and fear that much of the darkness is of one's own making. Since dark night is a limit experience, and since it does expose human fragility, brokenness, neurotic dependence, and lack of integration, it is understandable that it undermines a person's self-esteem and activates anxious self-analysis.

The only way to break out of this desperate circle of insoluble self-questioning is to surrender in faith and trust to the unfathomable Mystery that beckons onward and inward beyond calculation, order, self-justification, and fear. John continues, therefore:

> The third and surest sign is that a person likes to remain alone in loving awareness of God, without particular considerations, in interior peace and quiet and repose. . . .
>
> If those in whom this occurs know how to remain quiet, without care and solicitude about any interior or exterior work, they will soon in that unconcern and idleness delicately experience the interior nourishment.[24]

It is precisely as broken, poor, and powerless that one opens oneself to the dark mystery of God in loving, peaceful waiting. When the pain of human finitude is appropriated with consciousness and consent and handed over in one's own person to the influence of Jesus' spirit in the contemplative process, the new and deeper experience gradually takes over, the new vision slowly breaks through, and the new understanding and mutuality are progressively experienced.

At the deepest levels of night, in a way one could not have imagined it could happen, one sees the withdrawal of all one has been certain of and depended upon for reassurance and affirmation. Now it is a question, not of satisfaction, but of support systems that give life meaning: concepts, systems of meaning, symbolic structures, relationships, institutions. All supports seem to fail one, and only the experience of emptiness, confusion, isolation, weakness, loneliness, and abandonment remains. In the frantic search for reassurance, one wonders if anyone—friend or spouse or God—is really "for me," is trustworthy. But no answer is given to the question.[25]

The realization that there is *no* option but faith triggers a deep, silent, overpowering panic that, like a mighty underground river, threatens chaos and collapse. This "scream of suffering contains all the despair of which a person is capable, and in this sense every scream is a scream for God," writes Soelle.[26] In this experience of the cross of Jesus, what the "soul feels most," John explains, "is that God has rejected it and with abhorrence cast it into darkness."[27] And Soelle continues:

All extreme suffering evokes the experience of being forsaken by God. In the depth of suffering people see themselves as abandoned and forsaken by everyone. That which gave life its meaning has become empty and void: it turned out to be an error, an illusion that is shattered, a guilt that cannot be rectified, a void. The paths that lead to this experience of nothingness are diverse, but the experience of annihilation that occurs is the same.[28]

Yet it is the experience of this abandonment and rejection that is transforming the human person in love. This is a possession, a redemption, an actualizing and affirmation of the person that is not understood at the time. Its symbolic expression is dispossession and death.[29]

John seems to say that one leaves the world of rejection and worthlessness by giving away one's powerlessness and poverty to the inspiration of the Spirit and one moves into a world of self-esteem, affirmation, compassion, and solidarity. Only an experience like this, coming out of the soul's night, brings about the kind of solidarity and compassion that changes the "I" into a "we," enabling one to say, "we poor," "we oppressed," "we exploited." The poor are objects until we are poor, too. This kind of identification with God's people, with the "other," is the fruit of dark night.[30]

Some years ago it became evident to me that in our most significant human relationships we go through precisely the kind of suffering John describes concerning the soul's journey to God. In our ministries, moreover, we inevitably come to personal impasse. John's signs of passage and development, refashioned for the present time, should be a valuable tool for discernment. They relate to the breakdown of marriages, to departures from priesthood and religious life, and to the contemporary phenomenon of burnout, among other things.

SOCIETAL IMPASSE

I want to bring together dark night and societal impasse because, as I said, our experience of God and our spirituality must emerge from our concrete historical situation and because our time and place in history bring us face to face with profound societal impasse. Here God makes demands for conversion, healing, justice, love, compassion, solidarity, and communion. Here the face of God appears, a God who dies in human beings and rises in human freedom and dignity.

We close off the breaking in of God into our lives if we cannot admit into consciousness the situations of profound impasse we face personally and societally. If we deal with personal impasse only in the way our society teaches us—by illusion, minimization, repression, denial, apathy—we will deal with societal impasse in the same way. The "no way out" trials of our personal lives are but a part of the far more frightening situations of national and international impasse that have been formed by the social, economic, and political forces in our time.

We are citizens of a dominant nation, and I think that as a nation we have come to an experience of deep impasse and profound limitation. On the other side of all our technology, we have come to poverty and to dark night. We can find no escape from the world we have built, where the poor and oppressed cry out, where the earth and the environment cry out, and where the specter of nuclear waste already haunts future generations. We can find no way out of the horror of nuclear stockpiles but more sophisticated and deadly weapons systems.

As Americans we are not educated for impasse, for the experience of human limitation and darkness that will not yield to hard work, studies, statistics, rational analysis, and well-planned programs. We stand helpless, confused, and guilty before the insurmountable problems of our world. We dare not let the full import of the impasse even come to complete consciousness. It is just too painful and too destructive of national self-esteem. We cannot bear to let ourselves be totally challenged by the poor, the elderly, the unemployed, refugees, the oppressed; by the unjust, unequal situation of women in a patriarchal, sexist culture; by those tortured and imprisoned and murdered in the name of national security; by the possibility of the destruction of humanity.

We see only signs of death. Because we do not know how to read these kinds of signs in our own inner lives and interpersonal relationships, we do not understand them in our societal or national life, either. Is it possible these insoluble crises are signs of passage or transition in our national development and in the evolution of humanity? Is it possible we are going through a fundamental evolutionary change and transcendence, and crisis is the birthplace and learning process for a new consciousness and harmony?

Let us examine the signs. Our impasses do not yield to hard, generous work, to the logical solutions of the past, to the knowledge and skills acquired in our educational institutions. The most farsighted economists said some years ago that the economic solutions of past decades do not fit the present economic crisis in the world. It is argued that the whole economic, social, and political system would collapse were we to feed the poor with surplus crops and stop the wars, the exploitation, the oppression, in which we are involved. Not only God and the loved one fail us, our institutions fail us.

We are obsessed with the problem and with the need for new insight and breakthrough; we are disillusioned with a political system that contributes to international oppression, violence, and darkness. Is it any wonder we witness the effects of impasse among us—anger, confusion, violence—since real impasse or dark night highlights destructive tendencies? Frustrated desire fights back.

Recently, a Jesuit on our local Peace and Justice Commission described the stance of a prominent Roman Catholic theologian, a layman, at a meeting of theologians, bishops, and others on the nuclear question. It was the focused awareness, the incredible logic and rationality, of this man who favored nuclear superiority and denied that a nuclear freeze was a good idea that made such a negative impression on pro-freeze participants. Reason, left to itself, moved to a basically destructive position, unrecognized and unacknowledged in the speaker.

Dark night shows up the "shadow," the dark side of desire. If we refuse to read the signs of dark night in our society and avoid appropriating the impasse, we see cold reason, devoid of imagination, heading with deadly logic toward violence, hardness in the face of misery, a sense of inevitability, war, and death. And we witness the projection of our national shadow on others, "the inevitable shadow of over-rational planning," as Irene de Castillejo calls it.[31]

Today, instead of realizing that the impasse provides a challenge and concrete focus for prayer and drives us to contemplation, we give in to a passive sense of inevitability, and imagination dies. We do not really believe that if we surrender these situations of world impasse to contemplative prayer that new solutions, new visions of peace and equality, will emerge in our world. We dare not believe that a creative re-visioning of our world is possible. Everything is just too complex, too beyond our reach. Yet it is only in the process of bringing the impasse to prayer, to the perspective of the God who loves us, that our society will be freed, healed, changed, brought to paradoxical new visions, and freed for nonviolent, selfless, liberating action, freed, therefore, for community on this planet earth. Death is involved here—a dying in order to see how to be and to act on behalf of God in the world.[32]

This development suggests two questions: Do we really expect anything at all of the contemplative process of prayer in our world today? And how does the failure of imagination and creativity in our national life relate to the breakdown of the contemplative process of prayer and transformation in people's lives? With these questions concerning the intersection of impasse and contemplation, I move into my concluding reflection, on women's religious experience today.

FEMININE IMPASSE

I submit that the feminine experience of dark night, if we read it, interpret it, understand it, and live it through, is in itself a critique of religious consciousness and, therefore, ultimately of Christianity, with its roots in a sexist, patriarchal culture. It is not my intention simply to apply a Christian theme, dark night, to a contemporary issue, women. Rather, I am probing a resource within the theological-mystical tradition in order to understand the contemporary feminist experience of God and to see if John of the Cross' dark night can function in the struggle of women for liberation and equality.[33]

Behind every new spirituality and any creative re-visioning of the world—at the root of any real theology—is an experience of God. Yet every religious experience comes from a meeting with a new and challenging face of God in one's own time and social situation. I suspect that although it is imperative, for example, for feminist theologians to develop new interpretive paradigms that function to liberate people, only women's *experience* of God can alter or renew our God images and perhaps our doctrine of God. I want, therefore, to examine the feminist experience of God in impasse, because this is where many women in the Church, and in the world, find themselves. "We have only begun to experience the depth of women's alienation from Christian belief systems and from the existing Churches," writes Elisabeth Schüssler Fiorenza.[34]

Today feminists struggle with the Judeo-Christian image of a male God and a male Church. Just as Marxism sees religion as the opiate of the people and Christianity's doctrine of God as a support of oppression and misery, so the feminists see a patriarchal system that visualizes God, and consequently Church, in almost exclusively patriarchal terms as basically destructive. The masculine image of God is experienced as unsatisfying and confusing because it serves to reinforce male domination, a patriarchal value system, and an entire male world view.

This is an impasse for women, since their past religious experience has come to them through these images and this inherited symbol system, which does not function for women now as it did before. There is no going back to what was—what gave comfort and clarity and brought feminists to their present stage of religious development and commitment—but there is no satisfactory going forward either. There seems to be no way out of this God-less situation because no genuine evolution of God images has really occurred. We touch this in Alice Walker's latest novel, *The Color Purple*, a story of a black woman, Celie, who moves from being oppressed and brutalized to self-actualization and religious transformation. What is significant is that Celie's transcendence requires or coincides with a radical redefinition of God. "The author's choice of the genre of the epistolary novel, in this case composed entirely of letters for which there is no direct response," places the whole story in a prayer context.[35] In the first fifty-five letters Celie writes the story of her life to God, because she is ashamed to talk to him about it. Abused by the man she thought to be her father and deprived by him of the children she consequently bore, dehumanized by her husband and deprived by him of any knowledge of or communication with her sister, she is loved by one woman, Shug Avery. Aware finally, under the influence of Shug's love and affirmation, of the extent of her exploitation, Celie rebels not only against men but against God and can no longer write to *him*. She writes instead to her sister:

What God do for me? I ast. . . . He give me a lynched daddy, a crazy mama, a lowdown dog of a step pa and a sister I probably won't ever see again. Anyhow, I say, the God I been praying and writing to is a man. And act just like all the mens I know. Trifling, forgitful and lowdown. . . .

All my life I never care what people thought bout nothing I did, I say. But deep in my heart I care about God. What he going to think. And come to find out, he don't think. Just sit up there glorying in being deef, I reckon. But it ain't easy, trying to do without God. Even if you know he ain't there, trying to do without him is a strain.

When Shug asks what her God looks like, Celie senses the incongruity of her image but replies:

He big and old and tall and graybearded and white. He wear white robes and go barefooted.

Blue eyes? she ast.

Sort of bluish gray. Cool. Big though. White lashes, I say. . . . Ain't no way to read the bible and not think God white, she say. Then she sigh. When I found out I thought God was white, and a man, I lost interest. You mad cause he don't seem to listen to your prayers. Humph! Do the mayor listen to anything the colored say? . . . Here's the thing, say Shug. The thing I believe. God is inside you and inside everybody else. You come into the world with God. But only them that search for *it* inside find it. And sometimes it just manifest itself even if you not looking, or don't know what you looking for. Trouble do it for most folks, I think.

. . . [U]s talk and talk about God, but I'm still adrift. Trying to chase that old man out of my head. I been so busy thinking bout him I never truly notice nothing God make. Not a blade of corn (how it do that?) not the color purple (where it come from?) Not the little wildflowers. Nothing.

Man corrupt everything, say Shug. He on your box of grits, in your head and all over your radio. He try to make you think he everywhere. Soon as you think he everywhere, you think he God. But he ain't. Whenever you trying to pray, and man plop himself on the other end of it, tell him to git lost, say Shug. Conjure up flowers, wind, water, a big rock.

But this is hard work, let me tell you. He been there so long, he don't want to budge. He threaten lightening, floods and earthquakes. Us fight. I hardly pray at all. Every time I conjure up a rock, I throw it. Amen.[36]

Thus feminists, unable to communicate with the God of patriarchy, are imprisoned in a night of broken symbols. They ask how the idea of God undergoes transformation.

Is it by changing our religious language? By feminizing God, uncovering feminine images and attributes of God in the Scriptures? Is it by the desexualization of God and a move toward deism? Or is it by contemplation? (A step in the criticism of Marxism is implied here. Can experience really be altered simply by changing language?) What our programs to eliminate sexist language in our theological, devotional, and liturgical life have shown us is that our solutions are unsatisfactory and confusing. We find impasse not only in the problems but even in the solutions.

So-called postpatriarchal theologians and philosophers have suspected this for some time and in consequence have moved beyond Judeo-Christian religion. These radical feminist thinkers claim feminine consciousness and Christian faith are contradictions in terms. Aware, like John of the Cross, of the tendency of religion to become projection, they have rejected the Christian God that patriarchy projects. But is this the only option? Here the advance of postpatriarchy intersects with the development of contemplation. If one admits that religious belief and desire can be analyzed into episodes of projection, does the force of this discovery indicate a movement toward the total rejection of the God of patriarchy, or can it equally indicate that faith and desire must move into contemplation, one movement of which is apophatic? Is the alternative either to deny the reality of the God of Christianity or to insist that the evolution of faith and desire must pass through the darkness and the cross, in which the meaning of the night is found? It is imperative to emphasize, as Buckley observes,

that apophatic theology is not primarily one which does or does not make statements about God. It is primarily an experiential *process*, a process of entering into the infinite mystery that is God, so that gradually one is transformed by grace and this grace moves through the intense experience of darkness [impasse] into the *vision* of the incomprehensible God [the God who transcends present images and symbols]. Apophatic theology involves both interpretation and criticism, conceptualization and theological argument. But all of these are descriptive of *a process in which one is engaged*, a process in which *one must be engaged* in order to grasp its interpretation in any depth.[37]

If the impasse in which feminists find themselves *is* dark night, then a new experience of God, transformative of alienating symbols, is already breaking through even though it is not comprehensible yet, and impasse is a call to development, transcendence, new life, and understanding. Ultimately, therefore, impasse is a challenge to feminists to be mystics who, when human concepts disillusion, symbols break, and meanings fail, will let their "faith . . . relocate everything known within a new horizon in which it is radically reinterpreted and transvaluated."[38] Feminists need to realize that the gap that exists between human, patriarchal concepts of God and what is internalized by them in impasse is exactly what promises religious development and is the seed of a new experience of God, a new spirituality, and a new order—what Elizabeth Janeway calls the "Great Myth, as yet unborn," to which Madonna Kolbenschlag refers in her article, "Feminists, the Frog Princess, and the New Frontier of Spirituality."[39]

I believe there is no alternative for feminists except contemplation, if they are to avoid the trivialization of their own religious experience in dark night. The experience of God in impasse is the crucible in which our God images and language will be transformed and a feminine value system and social fabric generated. All the signs (of dark night) indicate this is the next step in any positive, creative re-visioning of the future, in any genuinely feminine generativity. Theology is dependent on this experience, which cannot be created by theological reflection alone. Dark night is, as was stated before, "a progressive hermeneutic of the nature of God." If this passage is not recognized and traversed, a certain kind of atheism and permanent cynicism are inevitable.

The contemplative love experience, which is beyond conscious control and is not given on demand, is concerned not for the image of God, as political theologians are, but with God, who does in the end transcend our images and expectations. What is critical to see is that one has to *allow* the experience to take place through a love that is gradually welling up from the ground of one's being and that serves as a basis for contemplation. Only this experience can give to theology the insight it needs "to search out a new doctrine of God which is related to the intellectual, practical, and ethical concerns of the present situation of women and which suggests transformation or emancipative possibilities for the future."[40]

Contemplation, and ultimately liberation, demand the handing over of one's powerlessness and "outsider-ness" to the inspiration and power of God's Spirit. How imperative it is that women take possession of their pain and confusion; actively appropriate their experience of domination, exploitation, and oppression; consent to their time in history; and hold this impasse in their bodies and their hearts before the inner God they reach for in the dark of shattered symbols. Although the God of the dark night seems silent, this God is not a mute God who silences human desire, pain, and feeling, and women need to realize that the experience of anger, rage, depression, and abandonment is a constitutive part of the transformation and purification of the dark night. This very rage and anger purify the "abused consciousness" of women in the sexism they have internalized.[41]

If there is, as we suggest, an incipient experience of God,

this presence of God will necessarily throw light on woman's "shadow" and reveal her to herself with all the destructive power she has and all the repressed possibilities or "lost alternatives" that cry within her for a voice. It is in the experience of this kind of night, when women put all the power of their desire, not in ideology, but here before the inner God, that the real bonding of women takes place, and purified of violence, they are readied for communion with their God, for sisterhood, equality, liberation, and mutuality.

Impasse internalizes the option for the poor and effects an identification with and compassion for all "women whose cry for liberation is so basic and unmistakable that it shouts out for all of us in our common quest for equality."[42] In one's own womanhood, one holds every woman before God, women of the present and women of the past. This is an experience, not a theory! Though one lives in Baltimore or Atlanta or California or Washington, one's life is lived within the bleeding borders of El Salvador and Guatemala, Lebanon and South Africa, Afghanistan and Cambodia. Though one lives at the end of the twentieth century, the voiceless sorrow of women long dead is felt as one's own. One senses this in Alice Walker's essay "In Search of Our Mother's Gardens":

When Jean Toomer walked through the South in the early twenties, he discovered a curious thing: Black women whose spirituality was so intense, so deep, so *unconscious*, that they themselves were unaware of the riches they held. They stumbled blindly through their lives: creatures so abused and mutilated in body, so dimmed and confused by pain, that they considered themselves unworthy even of hope. In the selfless abstractions their bodies became to the men who used them, they became more than "sexual objects," more even than mere women: they became Saints. Instead of being perceived as whole persons, their bodies became shrines: what was thought to be their minds became temples suitable for worship. These crazy "saints" stared out at the world, wildly, like lunatics—or quietly like suicides; and the "God" that was in their gaze was as mute as a great stone. . . .

. . . [T]hese grandmothers and mothers of ours were not "saints," but Artists; driven to a numb and bleeding madness by the springs of creativity in them for which there was no release. They were Creators who lived lives of spiritual waste, because they were so rich in spirituality—which is the basis for Art—that the strain of enduring their unused and unwanted talent drove them insane. Throwing away this spirituality was the pathetic attempt to lighten the soul to a weight the work-worn sexually abused bodies could bear.[43]

Such a time is past: the time of throwing away one's spirituality in order to survive.

It is regrettable that the possible liabilities of dark night theology cannot be dealt with in full here. Although some *interpretations* of dark night could reinforce passivity and women's internalized inferiority, subordination, lack of self-esteem and self-actualization, John of the Cross sings of the affirmation of the person by God within and of the redemption or transformation of affectivity that dark night effects. Dark contemplation is not a validation of things as they are or a ploy to keep women contented "outcasts of the [patriarchal] land"[44] but a constant questioning and restlessness that waits for and believes in the coming of a transformed vision of God; an affirmation of the self as woman that comes from deep inside and the consequent maturing to wholeness as a complete person; and a new and integrating spirituality capable of creating a new politics and generating new social structures.

Contemplation is what Dorothée Soelle calls revolutionary patience and is the epitome of passionate desire, activity, self-direction, autonomy, and bondedness.[45] It is a time bomb and will explode in new abilities and energy in women that cannot be conquered. Ultimately, it is the mystic, the contemplative woman, who will be reassured, affirmed, and loved, who will see and love, and for whose sake the world will be given sight, language, reassurance, and love. And she will understand Celie's final epistle, a letter to God: "Dear God. Dear stars, dear trees, dear sky, dear peoples. Dear Everything. Dear God."

NOTES

1. See David Tracy, *The Analogical Imagination, Christian Theology and the Culture of Pluralism* (New York: Crossroads, 1981), chap. 3, "The Classic."
2. Not only Tracy has influenced my methodology, but also Thomas H. Groome, *Christian Religious Education* (San Francisco, Harper & Row, 1980), pp. 185–222, and John Shea, *Stories of Faith* (Chicago: Thomas More Press, 1980), pp. 76–90. These three studies are helpful in dealing with the dialogue between tradition and contemporary story or issues.
3. Belden C. Lane, "Spirituality and Political Commitment: Notes on a Liberation Theology of Nonviolence," *America*, March 14, 1981; see also Urban T.

Holmes III, *Ministry and Imagination* (New York: Seabury, 1981), pp. 89–93, for a good treatment of right- and left-brain thinking. Holmes works out of the contributions of Jerome S. Bruner, *On Knowing: Essays for the Left Hand* (New York: Atheneum, 1971), and Robert E. Ornstein, *The Psychology of Consciousness* (New York: Viking, 1972), pp. 57–64.

4. Dorothée Soelle, *Suffering* (Philadelphia: Fortress, 1975), p. 36.
5. See ibid., pp. 76, 11.
6. Lane, "Spirituality and Political Commitment," p. 198. Lane's discussion of the theory of Paul Witzalawick, John Weakland, and Richard Fisch in *Change: Principles of Problem Formation and Problem Resolution* (New York: Norton, 1974).
7. There are other models to explain and verify this experience: e.g., the creative process as it is described by Ralph J. Hallman, "Aesthetic Pleasure and Creative Process," *Humanitas* 4 (1968), pp. 161–68, or *Journal of Humanistic Psychology* 6 (1966), pp. 141–47; the process of individuation developed by Carl Jung and described by John Welch, O. Carm., *Spiritual Pilgrims: Carl Jung and Teresa of Avila* (New York: Paulist Press, 1982), esp. pp 136–37, 141–43, 151–62; the model of structure and anti-structure developed by Victor W. Turner, *The Forest of Symbols: Aspects of Ndembu Ritual* (Ithaca: Cornell University Press, 1967), pp. 93–101, *The Ritual Process: Structure and Anti-Structure* (Chicago: Aldine, 1969), *Dramas, Fields and Metaphors: Symbolic Action in Human Society* (Ithaca: Cornell University Press, 1974). See Holmes, *Ministry and Imagination*, pp. 119–36, for material on Turner's structure and anti-structure.
8. See John of the Cross, *The Collected Works of St. John of the Cross*, trans. Kieran Kavanaugh and Otilio Rodriguez (Washington, D.C.: Institute of Carmelite Studies, 1973), *Ascent of Mount Carmel*, Book I, chap. 13, no. 3; chap. 14, no. 2; poem, "The Dark Night," p. 296; poem, "The Spiritual Canticle," pp. 410–15; *The Dark Night*, Book II, chap. 9, no. 1; *The Living Flame*, stanza 3, nos. 1,3,7.
9. See John of the Cross, *CW*, *The Dark Night*, Book I, chaps. 1–8, for a view of the dark side of human desire. John calls this dark side the faults of beginners.
10. See Michael J. Buckley, "Atheism and Contemplation," *Theological Studies* 40 (1979), p. 696; see also John of the Cross, *CW*, *The Spiritual Canticle*, stanzas 3–7, to grasp how one moves through that which one cherishes—the self, the world, relationships—to deeper love for God.
11. See John of the Cross, *CW*, *The Dark Night*, Book I, chap. 7, no. 5; chap. 8, no. 3.
12. See ibid., Book I, chap. 9, no. 4.
13. For the first set of signs, see ibid., Book I, chap. 9, no. 8; *Ascent of Mount Carmel*, Book II, chap. 13, no. 2.
14. John, *CW*, *The Dark Night*, Book I, chap. 9, no. 7.
15. Ibid., Book I, chap. 8, no. 3.
16. Buckley, "Atheism and Contemplation," p. 694.
17. Ibid., p. 693, see also p. 690.
18. John, *CW*, *The Dark Night*, Book I, chap. 16, no. 2.
19. Buckley, "Atheism and Contemplation," p. 694.
20. Ibid. pp. 696–97.
21. See John, *CW*, *The Dark Night*, Book I, chap. 9, no. 2; for correlating signs, see also *Ascent of Mount Carmel*, Book II, chap. 13, no. 3.
22. See John, *CW*, *The Dark Night*, Book I, chap. 14, where he speaks of the spirit of fornication, blasphemy, and confusion (*spiritus vertiginis*), or what I would

call frustrated desire. See also Welch, *Spiritual Pilgrims*, pp. 141–46.

23. John, *CW, The Dark Night*, Book I, chap. 9, no. 3.

24. John, *CW, Ascent of Mount Carmel*, Book II, chap. 13, no. 4; *The Dark Night*, Book I, chap. 6, no.2.

25. See Welch, *Spiritual Pilgrims*, p. 145.

26. Soelle, *Suffering*, p. 85.

27. John, *CW, Ascent of Mount Carmel*, Book II, chap. 6, no. 2.

28. Soelle, *Suffering*, p. 85.

29. See Buckley, "Atheism and Contemplation," p. 696.

30. See Constance FitzGerald, "Contemplative Life as Charismatic Presence," *Contemplative Review* 11 (1978), p. 45, or *Spiritual Life* 29 (1983), p. 28.

31. See Irene Claremont de Castillejo, *Knowing Woman: A Feminine Perspective* (New York: Harper & Row, 1974), pp. 32, 39; see also pp. 17–18 for a very interesting analysis of the different levels on which people discuss nuclear weapons.

32. See Holmes, *Ministry and Imagination*, p. 154. The entire chapter 6, "Dying to Image," pp. 137–164, is excellent supplementary reading to my development.

33. See Anne Carr, B.V.M., "Is a Christian Feminist Theology Possible?" *Theological Studies* 43 (1982), pp. 282, 292; Elisabeth Schüssler Fiorenza, "Toward a Feminist Biblical Hermeneutics: Biblical Interpretation and Liberation Theology," *The Challenge of Liberation Theology*, ed. Mahan, p. 109: "Theological interpretation must also critically reflect on the political presuppositions and implications of theological 'classics' and dogmatic or ethical systems. In other words, not only the content and traditioning process within the Bible, but the whole of Christian tradition should be scrutinized and judged as to whether or not it functions to oppress or liberate people."

34. Elisabeth Schüssler Fiorenza, "Sexism and Conversion," *Network* (May–June 1981), p. 21.

35. Sue E. Houchins, "I Found God in Myself/And I Loved Her/I Loved Her Fiercely: A Study of Suffering in the Archetypal Journey of Alice Walker's Female Heroes," a chapter of a dissertation in progress. p. 15.

36. Alice Walker, *The Color Purple* (New York: Harcourt Brace Jovanovich, 1982), 164–168.

37. Buckley, "Atheism and Contemplation," p. 690. (italics mine).

38. Ibid. p. 695.

39. Quoted by Madonna Kolbenschlag, "Feminists, The Frog Princess, and the New Frontier of Spirituality," *New Catholic World*, July–August 1982.

40. Carr, "Is a Christian Feminist Theology Possible?" p. 293.

41. Here I am addressing the call of Fiorenza for "a spirituality that understands anger, persecution, defamation, violence and suffering in political-theological terms." See "Sexism and Conversion," pp. 20–21.

42. Maureen Fiedler, "The Equal Rights Amendment and the Bonding of Women," *LCWR Newsletter* 8 (1980), p. 5.

43. Alice Walker, "In Search of Our Mother's Gardens," in *Working It Out*, ed. Sara Rudick and Pamela Daniels (New York: Pantheon 1977), p. 93.

44. Houchins, "I Found God in Myself," quoted from Anne Pratt, *Archetypal Patterns in Women's Fiction* (Bloomington, Ind.: Indiana University Press, 1981), 5.

45. Dorothée Soelle, *Revolutionary Patience* (Maryknoll, N.Y.: Orbis, 1977); see also Marianne Katoppo, *Compassionate and Free: An Asian Woman's Theology* (Maryknoll, N.Y.: Orbis, 1980), p. 21.

7. Despair and Empowerment Work

JOANNA ROGERS MACY

I would like to tell you about a work, or ministry, that deals with the challenge of "living with apocalypse." It has risen in response to the denial, despair, and powerlessness gripping many of us as we face global suffering and the threat of mass annihilation. The main obstacles to effective concerted action to avert disaster and heal our world are not technical or even political so much as psychological. This work I will tell you about helps us break through these obstacles and awaken to both the peril and the promise of our time on this planet. It helps us rediscover our passion and compassion, our deep capacities to care, to connect, and to act.

Since 1979 thousands of people across the country and abroad have engaged in this work and found it helpful in releasing their energies on behalf of humanity. These workshops are usually called "Despairwork" or "Despair and Empowerment" or "Awakening in the Nuclear Age." For them, I draw on general systems theory and also on religious teachings—especially on the biblical and Buddhist traditions, since these have shaped most strongly my own life and thought and those of my closest colleagues. Indeed, the work can be seen in part as a new application of these ancient spiritual paths.

To tell you about this work, I will describe briefly (1) the presence and repression of our pain for the world; (2) the nature of despair and empowerment work; (3) its spiritual roots; and (4) some useful meditative practices.

OUR PAIN FOR THE WORLD

"It's too horrible to think about. I just block it out."

"Everything I do seems pointless. It could all go at any time."

"Maybe a nuclear war *can* be limited. Maybe we'll survive."

"If it happens, it happens. I just hope it's quick."

"I don't think about world-hunger—or acid rain—because there's nothing I can do about it."

"I think about it all the time and do everything I can. But I still feel terrible because it doesn't seem enough."

"I don't read the news anymore. I don't want to spoil the time I have left."

Premonitions of apocalypse are widespread in our society, as these common responses suggest. A sense of foreboding, of living on the brink of time, touches all of us, regardless of political persuasion or walk of life. For to be conscious in our world today means to be aware of unprecedented peril. This peril comes from three developments: Each is of catastrophic proportions; each increases daily in intensity; and each has become a standard feature in our psychic landscape. You know them:

The growing threat of nuclear holocaust. Our country bases its power and policy on the credibility of this threat. And it looms so real that the majority of Americans queried in polls state that they expect to die in a nuclear war. (How many minutes has it taken you to read this far? Each minute a million dollars is poured into the arms race.)

The progressive deterioration of our life-support system. Toxic wastes with thermal, chemical, and radioactive pollution; destruction of topsoil, forestland, water reserves, species of plant and animal life—all increase at exponential rates. If this continues, according to scientists' extrapolations, our planet will be uninhabitable in another generation.

The growing misery of half the planet's people. Perhaps never has so large a proportion of humanity been without the means for a healthy and decent life. With the widening gap between "haves" and "have-nots" and with the spread of dictatorship, detention, and torture, we see injustice on a grotesquely mammoth scale. It triggers rage that turns our planet into a tinderbox.

We are aware of these developments because they bombard us in each day's news. Barraged by signals of human and planetary distress, we are prey to an inchoate anguish for our world and its future. It is compounded of fear, rage, sorrow, and guilt; and no one is immune.

Yet this widespread sense of anguish remains below the surface. Because of fear of pain and because of social taboos against expressions of despair, most of us stifle our innermost response to the portents of apocalypse. In a culture that prizes optimism and admonishes us to "keep smiling," we tend to hide it like a secret shame, fearing that we will fall apart if we let ourselves fully experience it and be ostracized if we openly express it. For Americans, citizens of a nation built on utopian hopes, it can seem even unpatriotic to entertain feelings of despair. For Christians it can seem tantamount to a lapse of faith. "God won't let it happen," we say—and bury our anxieties, stopping our ears to cries of alarm. We have been conditioned, furthermore, to separate self from other, thought from feeling. We dismiss onslaughts of pain for the world as "just" feelings, subjective and morbid, stemming perhaps from some personal maladjustment. Thus do we push down and deny the very responses we most have in common.

This repression results in "psychic numbing," a term coined by psychiatrist Robert J. Lifton in his study of Hiroshima survivors. He now finds it affecting all of us, confronted as we are with future possibilities too horrifying to contemplate. In consequence we lead, he says, a "double life": on the surface preoccupying ourselves with business-as-usual while in the depths of consciousness lurk dreads too terrible to name or face.

Repression of social despair, like that of any strong, recurrent emotion, takes a heavy toll. It blurs our thinking and drains us of energy urgently required for creative response. It fosters resistance to the information we most need to deal with, blocking feedback and breeding a sense of unreality, isolation, and powerlessness. Furthermore, as Freud pointed out in what he termed "the return of the repressed," denied material surfaces in other ways. Unacknowledged despair for the world and its future erupts in violence—which is either turned outward against society in aggression and vandalism or inward in acts of self-destruction, as the rising rates of drug abuse and suicide attest. In either case, repression of feeling severs the nerve between knowledge and appropriate action. We *know* the danger but tend to act as if we did not. For example, though polls show that well over 50 percent of the public anticipate a nuclear war within their lifetime—and do not expect that they or civilization will survive it—few speak out in rage and protest, and not one of our planet's fifty thousand nuclear weapons, poised on hair-trigger alert, has yet been dismantled.

All this makes clear that public apathy does not stem from indifference or from ignorance of the dangers facing us; it derives, rather, from dread—or, more precisely, from reluctance to confront and experience this dread. It is born, not out of callousness, but out of confusion about how to accept and deal with our pain for the world.

THE PRACTICAL PROCESS

When dealt with on the cognitive level alone, the dangers facing us are, as William Sloane Coffin puts it, "too ghastly to take seriously." If we are to overcome denial and avoidance, we must deal with them on the psychological and spiritual level as well. By permitting ourselves to acknowledge and share our social despair, seeing it as a normal, healthy human response, we can move through it and tap vast inner resources for creative, effective action.

To allow this to happen, it is good to have a safe setting, removed temporarily from the distractions and pressures of daily life. And it is helpful to have a leader or facilitator to set the theme and tone, validating our feelings of pain for the world as worthy human responses. A quiet relaxation of breath and body helps us to "center" and to open to the voices within. The facilitator may begin, as I usually do, by inviting those gathered to recall some incident in the last week or so that caused them pain for their world. It could be a news item, an encounter, or a dream. This is then shared with the others in small groups—no one is at a loss for something to recount. When this sharing is completed, I invite the participants to observe that each incident shared involves concerns that extend beyond the separate ego, beyond our individual needs and wants. This I say, tells us something of great importance about who and what we are.

The very process of owning and expressing our pain for the world—our apprehensions for the planet, for those living on it now and those yet unborn—releases us from isolation. It also permits us to make certain discoveries about our true nature as human beings. For as we accept and move through our pain, we come to its source, which is caring. There we rediscover our intrinsic interconnectedness. It is a kind of homecoming.

As the group work progresses, we engage in a variety of exercises. We tell our "nuclear stories," reviewing and recounting our lives from the perspective of our unfolding awareness of the world's distress. We also use silence and sound, music and movement and colors on paper, to explore the depths of our pain for the world, breaking our culture's taboo against expressions of despair. We enter into guided meditations and rituals to experience how this pain can open us to power. For this pain, we learn, is nothing other than compassion, "suffering with." It is rooted in our interconnectedness as members of one body or nerve cells in one neural net. The power then available to us stems from the same source; it is the synergy of our interexistence. It comes to us from beyond the confines of our skin, beyond the ordinary constructs of self, as we open to wider dimensions of being. We see how this power is available to us when we act on behalf of humanity and on behalf of the planet. And we prepare ourselves to use it for the healing of our world. We emerge with a keener and vaster sense of community and with the courage and commitment that brings.

As many have attested, despair work can be undertaken alone, especially with some written materials as a guide. But group work is particularly effective. In interaction we can experience more immediately the depth and universality of our pain for the world—and recognize it as living proof of our interconnectedness. We do not emerge purged of this pain so much as integrated with it, ready to let it widen and transform our lives.

For those who are already committed to social action, this process helps avoid emotional exhaustion, or "burnout." Since the approach is apolitical, cutting across ideological boundaries to deal on the affective level, it also reaches people whose despair includes the fact that they are in direct service to the military-industrial complex. Validated in their deepest responses to the crises of our time, participants in despair work—whether undertaken in town halls or church basements—go on to take action and risk on behalf of the wider humanity they now sense as inseparable from their inner selves.

SPIRITUAL ROOTS

Even in so brief a sketch of despair and empowerment work, its spiritual roots and dimensions can be surmised. Every major religion calls us to move beyond the confines of egocentricity; each summons us to recognize the depth of our community with all fellow beings. The work not only draws from spiritual teachings, it also serves as a vehicle for them.

My own journey in developing this work has been shaped by the two traditions that I have most learned from and loved: the biblical and the Buddhist. As I experience them, both begin existentially with the undeniable fact of suffering. For the Buddha it was the First Noble Truth; for the prophets of the Old Testament and Jesus himself on the cross, it was a painful gift, to be embraced and transformed. Neither tradition shies away from the fact of suffering; neither wishes it away. Hence the measure of their human vitality and authority. Suffering exists. Cruelty and conflict and injustice exist. How to encompass them? What meanings to wrestle from them? How to respond? In standing before these questions, I'll speak first as a Christian and then as a Buddhist.

As a Christian, I learned that the willingness to suffer pain on behalf of others—and on behalf of the whole of which we are a part—is a measure of willingness to engage in life. That willingness can be called love, but I don't relish what our culture has done with that word. For me this readiness has components of courage and venturing and knowing that sentimentalized "love" does not convey. Amos, Micah, Isaiah—they did not cry out for the poor and storm and weep out of sentiment so much as out of deep certainty that the griefs of one were the griefs of all. Through the Hebrew prophets comes the realization that opening to social suffering is transformative for both individual and society. It widens the heart while bringing to light the causes of this suffering in greed and injustice. In a sense, it *redeems* the suffering by letting it tell us what we most need to know. Instead of holding aloof from grief, this movement of entering and opening to grief turns it into a kind of resource.

This biblical understanding found its fullest expression in Jesus—in what he said and in the way he died. In his openness to the pain of the world, he saw that what was done "unto the least of these my brethren" was done also to him, and in that same openness he let the stupidity, hatred, and greed that cause this pain take their full toll on him and play out their act. In an ultimate kind of *tai chi*, he let these dark forces expend themselves on his wracked body and so reveal their intrinsic pettiness, their ultimate bankruptcy.

So we learn—or are asked to learn—to be unafraid of the dark, to pass through it as we share the pain of the world, so that our interconnectedness can be realized—reborn—anew. It is to that profound mutuality that we come home, seeing each other in a new light, as interlinked as synapses in the mind of God.

As a Buddhist I was helped to see the myriad tricks of mind that trap us in the delusion of separateness. By fears and wants and self-protective games, we shore up our little ego and turn it into a prison cell. The Buddha dharma offers ways of awakening and walking out of that cell. It teaches us to see the fluid, dynamic nature of our experiencing and to watch that experiencing so attentively that the needful, clamoring "I" goes still—and eventually transparent. No artificial walls then divide the world from the beholder, the knower from the known. Beyond dichotomies all comes into focus, held in the light of sheer awareness and compassion.

That compassion is portrayed in the life story of Gautama Buddha and in the many beloved *jataka* or birth tales that recount his earlier incarnations in human or animal form. Whether of the elephant king or the monkey, the rabbit or the Brahmin, each tale describes an act of extraordinary generosity, of self-offering and self-sacrifice for the sake of other beings. These acts convey the courage and compassion of the *bodhisattva,* the figure that emerged as the hero model of the Buddhist tradition. Although he or she is enlightened and could win through to ultimate release from the world of suffering, the bodhisattva turns back from the gates of Nirvana, vowing to take birth again and again until all beings are saved. By his compassion, says the Lotus Sutra, he is endowed with supranormal senses. He can hear the music of the spheres and understand the language of the birds. By the same token, by virtue of his extended sensitivity, he hears as well all cries of distress, even to the moaning of beings in the lowest level of hell. All griefs are registered and owned in the "boundless heart" of the bodhisattva and in his deep knowledge that we are not separate from each other. *"Let all sorrow ripen in me"* (Shantideva).

There is in Buddhism a keen respect for method, so the teachings offer practical techniques for enhancing our capacity to experience that "boundless heart." Instead of just admonishing people to love their fellow beings or to emulate the compassion of the bodhisattva, simple, step-by-step exercises are set forth showing how to do it. I have adapted and used a number of them in my despair and empowerment workshops. Many participants have proceeded to take them as an ongoing personal discipline. Geared to be used in the course of the activities and encounters of our daily lives, they remind us that we do not need to withdraw from the world or spend long hours in solitary prayer or meditation to begin to wake up to the spiritual power within us.

SPIRITUAL EXERCISES

The four practices that follow are presented in much the same fashion as they are in the workshops. There I point out that although they are derived from the Buddhist tradition, they belong to us all, as part of our planetary heritage. No belief system is necessary, only readiness to attend to the immediacy of our own experiencing. In written form, they are most useful when read with a quiet mind (a couple of deep breaths helps) and then put directly into practice in the presence of others.

DEATH MEDITATION

Most spiritual paths begin with the recognition of the transiency of human life. Medieval Christians honored this in the mystery play of *Everyman*. Don Juan, the Yaqui sorcerer, taught that the enlightened warrior walks with death at his shoulder. To confront and accept the inevitability of our dying releases us from attachments and frees us to live boldly.

An initial meditation on the Buddhist path involves reflection on the twofold fact that "Death is certain, and the time of death is uncertain." In our world today the thermonuclear bomb, serving in a sense as spiritual teacher, does that meditation for us, for we all know now that we can die together at any moment, without warning. When we deliberately let the reality of that possibility surface in our consciousness, it can, of course, be painful, but it also helps us rediscover some fundamental truths about life. It jolts us awake to life's vividness or "suchness," heightening our awareness of its beauty and of the uniqueness of each object, each being. In despair work participants have found that this recognition can seize us with more immediacy and power when it arises in relation to another being.

As an occasional practice in daily life: *Look at the person you encounter* (stranger, friend). *Let the realization arise in you that this person may die in a nuclear war. Keep breathing. Observe that face, unique, vulnerable. . . . Those eyes still can see; they are not empty sockets . . . the skin is still intact. . . . Become aware of your desire, as it arises, that this person be spared such horror and suffering; feel the strength of that desire. . . . Keep breathing. . . . Let the possibility arise in your consciousness that this may be the person you happen to be with when you die . . . that face the last you see . . . that hand the last you touch. . . . It might reach out to help you then, to comfort, to give water. . . . Open to the feelings for this person that surface in you with the awareness of this possibility. Open to the levels of caring and connection it reveals in you.*

"BREATHING THROUGH"

Famine, torture, toxic wastes, the arms race—our time assails us with painful information that must be internalized if we are to respond and survive. But how can we take it all in without being overwhelmed by its horror? How can we open to it without falling apart?

We can do it by experiencing ourselves as resilient patterns within a vaster web of knowing. As organic parts of the web of all life, we are like neurons in a neural net, through which flow currents of awareness of what is happening to us as a species and as a planet. These currents bring us pain as well as pleasure. If we deny our pain for the world, we become like blocked and atrophied neurons, deprived of life's vitality and weakening the larger body in which we take being. To the extent that we let it flow through us, we affirm our belonging; our collective awareness increases; we become like bodhisattvas. We will never perceive the full beauty of life if we close our eyes and ears to its suffering; suffering, stretching the heart-mind beyond the bounds of ego, builds the compassion without which wisdom fails.

The practice of "breathing through" can help us open to the world's suffering in ways that strengthen us by affirming our essential interconnectedness. It is adapted from an ancient Tibetan meditation for the development of compassion.

Relax. Center on your breathing. . . . Visualize your breath as a stream flowing up through your nose, down through windpipe, lungs. Take it down through your lungs and, picturing an opening in the bottom of your heart, visualize the breath-stream passing through your heart and out through that opening to reconnect with the larger web of life around you. Let the breath-stream, as it passes through you, appear as one loop within that vast web connecting you with it. . . .

Now open your awareness to the suffering that is present in the world. Drop for now all defenses and open to your knowledge of that suffering. . . . Let it come as concretely as you can . . . concrete images of your fellow beings in pain and need, in fear and isolation, in prisons, hospitals, tenements, refugee camps. . . . No need to strain for these images, they are present in you by virtue of our interexistence. Relax and just let them surface, breathe them in, breathe them through . . . the numberless hardships of our fellow humans and of our animal brothers and sisters, too, as they swim the seas and fly through the air of this ailing planet. . . . Breathe in that pain like a dark stream, up through your nose, down through your lungs and heart, and out again into the world net. . . .

You are asked to do nothing for now but let it pass through your heart. . . .
Keep breathing. . . . Be sure that stream flows through and out *again,*
don't hang on to the pain. Surrender it for now to the healing resources
of life's vast web. . . .

With Shantideva, the Buddhist saint, we can say, "Let all sorrows
ripen in me." We help them ripen by passing them through our hearts . . .
making good compost out of all that grief . . . so we can learn from it,
enhancing our larger, collective knowing. . . .

If you experience an ache in the chest, a pressure within the rib cage,
that is all right. The heart that breaks open can contain the whole
universe. Your heart is that large. Trust it. Keep breathing.

This guided meditation serves to introduce the process of
breathing through, which, once experienced, becomes useful in
daily life in the situations that confront us with painful information. By "breathing through" the bad news, rather than bracing
ourselves against it, we can let it strengthen our sense of belonging in the larger web of being. It helps us remain alert and open,
whether reading the newspaper, receiving criticism, or simply
being present to a person who suffers.

For activists working for peace and justice and those dealing
most directly with the griefs of our time the practice provides
protection from burnout. Reminding us of the collective nature
of both our problems and our power, it offers a healing measure
of humility. It can also save us from self-righteousness, for when
we can take in our world's pain, accepting it as the price of our
caring, we can let it inform our acts without needing to inflict it
as a punishment on others who appear to feel, at the moment,
less involved.

THE GREAT BALL OF MERIT

Compassion, which is grief with the griefs of others, is but one
side of the coin. The other side is joy in the joy of others, which
in Buddhism is called *muditha.* To the extent that we allow ourselves to identify with the sufferings of other beings, we can
identify as well with their strengths and good fortune. Buddhism, more than any other tradition, names and features this
powerful human capacity. Sometimes translated as altruistic or
sympathetic joy (our Western culture does not have a word for it
yet), *muditha* is the third of the four "abodes" of the Buddha,

along with lovingkindness, compassion, and equanimity. One way to develop it is through the mental practice of the Great Ball of Merit, which is drawn from the meditation on Jubilation and Transformation in one of the earliest Mahayana texts.

Like the notion of *muditha*, the Great Ball of Merit is particularly helpful to those of us who have been socialized in a competitive society based on the zero-sum or win-lose notion of power: "The more you have, the less I have." Conditioned by that one-way paradigm of power, we can fall prey to the stupidity of viewing the strengths or good fortunes of other beings as a sign of our inadequacy or deprivation. Beside the eloquent colleague we feel inarticulate, in the presence of an athlete we feel weak and clumsy; so doing we often come to resent both ourselves and the other person. The experience of *muditha* brings us home, with a vast sense of ease, to our capacity for mutual enjoyment and empowerment. It also expands our sense of the resources available to us as agents for social change, for this time of great challenge demands more commitment, courage, and endurance than we can ever dredge up out of our individual supply. We can learn to view the strengths of others, with celebration and gratitude, as so much "money in the bank."

The concept is similar to the Christian notion of grace, in which, recognizing our own limitations, we cease relying solely on our individual strength and open ourselves to the power that is beyond and can flow through us. The Buddhist Ball of Merit is useful in helping us see that this power or grace is not dependent on belief in God but operates as well through our fellow beings. In so doing, it lets us connect with each other more fully and appreciatively than we usually do. It also helps us, when we work together, to avoid the tensions bred by comparison and envy.

Among participants in despair work the practice takes two forms. The one closer to the ancient Buddhist meditation is this:

Close your eyes and relax into your breathing. . . . Open your awareness to the fellow beings who share with you this planet-time, in this room . . . this neighborhood . . . this town. . . . Open to all those in this country . . . and in other lands. . . . Let your awareness encompass all beings living now in our world. Opening now to all time as well, let your awareness encompass all beings who ever lived . . . of all races and creeds and walks of life, rich and poor, kings and beggars, saints and sinners. . . . Like successive mountain ranges, the vast ranks of these fellowbeings present themselves to your mind's eye. . . .

Now open yourself to the knowledge that in each of these innumerable lives some act of merit was performed. No matter how stunted or deprived the life, there was a gesture of generosity, a gift of love, an act of valor or self-sacrifice . . . on the battlefield or at the workplace, in hospital or home. . . . From each of these beings in their endless multitudes arose actions of courage or kindness, of teaching or healing. . . . Let yourself see these manifold and immeasurable acts of merit. . . . As they arise in your mind's eyes, sweep them together. . . . Sweep them into a pile in front of you. . . . Use your hands . . . Pile them up . . . Pile them into a heap. . . . Pat them into a ball. It is the Great Ball of Merit. . . . Hold it and weigh it in your hands. . . . Rejoice in it, knowing that no act of goodness is ever lost. It remains ever and always a present resource . . . a resource for the transformation of life. . . . And now, with jubilation and gratitude, you turn that great ball. . . . Turn it over . . . over . . . into the healing of our world.

As we can learn from modern science and picture in the holographic model of reality, our lives interpenetrate. In the fluid tapestry of space-time, there is at root no distinction between self and other. The acts and intentions of others are like seeds that can germinate and bear fruit through our own lives as we take them into awareness and dedicate, or "turn over," that awareness to our empowerment. Thoreau, Gandhi, Martin Luther King, Jr., Dorothy Day, and the nameless heroes and heroines of our own day—all can be part of our Ball of Merit on which we can draw for inspiration and endurance.

In a similar fashion, the second, more workaday version of the Ball of Merit meditation helps us experience the synergy of opening to the powers of others. This exercise focuses on the expectant attention we bring to our encounters with other beings, helping to view them with fresh openness and curiosity about how they can enhance our Ball of Merit. We can play that inner game at any time, whether looking at someone on the bus or at someone across the bargaining table. It is especially useful when dealing with someone with whom we may be in conflict.

What does this person add to my Great Ball of Merit? What gifts of intellect can enrich our common store? What reserves of stubborn endurance can she or he offer? What flights of fancy or powers of love lurk behind those eyes? What kindness or courage hides in those lips, what healing in those hands?

Then, as with the breathing-through exercise, we open ourselves to the presence of those strengths, inhaling our awareness of them. . . . As our awareness grows, we experience our gratitude for them and our capacity to partake, even to elicit and enhance.

In the light of the Great Ball of Merit, the gifts and good fortunes of others appear, not as challenges to competition, but as resources we can honor and take pleasure in. We can learn to play detective, spying out from even the unlikeliest material treasures for the enhancement of life. Like air and sun and water, they form part of our common good. In addition to releasing us from the mental cramp of envy, this spiritual practice—or game—offers two other rewards: One is pleasure in our own acuity, as our merit-detecting ability improves. The second is the response of others, who, though ignorant of the game we are playing, sense something in our manner that invites them to move more openly into the person they can be.

LEARNING TO SEE EACH OTHER

This exercise is derived from the Buddhist practice of the Four Abodes of the Buddha mentioned earlier—also known as the Brahmaviharas: lovingkindness, compassion, joy in the joy of others, and equanimity. In the Sarvodaya Movement for community development in Sri Lanka, these four powers are considered fundamental to social action. They, and especially the first of these, *metta,* are practiced in silent meditation at the outset of each meeting. In adapting them for use by Westerners, I have presented them as a mental exercise to be undertaken in direct social interaction; as such, they help us see each other more truly and experience the depths of our interconnection.

In workshops I offer this as a guided meditation, with participants sitting in pairs facing each other.

As you face each other without talking, take a couple of deep breaths, centering yourself and exhaling tension. Look into each other's eyes. If you feel discomfort or an urge to laugh or look away, just note that embarrassment with patience and gentleness toward yourself and come back, when you can, to your partner's eyes. You may never see this person again: The opportunity to behold the uniqueness of this particular human being is given to you now.

As you look into this being's eyes, let yourself become aware of the powers that are there. . . . Open your awareness to the gifts and strengths and potentialities in this being. . . . Behind those eyes are unmeasured reserves of ingenuity and endurance, of wit and wisdom. There are gifts there, of which this person her- or himself is unaware. Consider what these untapped powers can do for the healing of our planet and the relishing of our common life. . . . As you consider that, let yourself become aware of your desire that this person be free from fear. . . . Let yourself experience how much you want this being to be free from hatred . . . free from greed . . . free from confusion . . . free from sorrow and the causes of suffering. . . . Know that what you are now experiencing is the great lovingkindness: . . . It is good for building a world.

Now, as you look into those eyes, let yourself become aware of the pain that is there. There are sorrows accumulated in that life's journey. . . . There are failures and losses, griefs and disappointments, beyond the telling. . . . Let yourself open to them, open to that pain . . . to hurts that this person may never have shared with another being. . . . What you are now experiencing is the great compassion. . . . It is good for the healing of our world.

As you look into those eyes, open to the thought of how good it would be to make common cause. . . . Consider how ready you might be to work together . . . to take risks in a joint venture, sharing excitement, challenge, laughter . . . learning to trust each other and acting boldly. . . . As you open to that possibility, what you open to is the great wealth: the pleasure in each other's powers, the joy in each other's joy.

Lastly now, let your consciousness drop deep within you like a stone, sinking below the level of what words or acts can express. . . . Breathe quietly. . . . Open your awareness to the deep web of interrelationship that underlies and interweaves all experiencing, all knowing. . . . It is the web of life in which you both have taken being . . . in which you are supported. . . . Out of that vast web you cannot fall. No stupidity or failure, no personal inadequacy, can ever sever you from that living web, for that is what you are . . . like a synapse in the mind of God. . . . Feel the assurance of that knowledge. Feel the great peace . . . rest in it. . . . Out of that great peace, we can venture everything. We can trust. We can act.

At the close of this meditation, I encourage participants to use it, or any portion of it they like, as they go about the business of their daily lives. It is an excellent antidote to boredom when our mind is idling and our eye falls on another person—say on the bus or in a checkout line—it charges that idle moment with beauty and discovery. It is also useful when dealing with people we are tempted to dislike or disregard, for it breaks open our accustomed ways of viewing them. When used like this, as a meditation in action, one does not, of course, gaze long and deeply into the other's eyes, as in the guided exercise. A seemingly casual glance is enough, or the simple exchange of buying stamps or toothpaste—any occasion, in other words, that permits us to be present to another human being.

In doing it we realize that we do not have to be particularly noble or saintlike in order to wake up to the power of our oneness with other beings. In our time, that simple awakening is the gift the Bomb holds for us; for all its horror and stupidity, it is the manifestation of an awesome spiritual truth, the truth about the hell we create for ourselves when we cease to learn how to love. For us to regard the Bomb (or the dying seas, the poisoned air) as a monstrous injustice to us would suggest that we never took seriously the injunction to love. Perhaps we thought all along that the teachings of Gautama or Jesus were meant only for saints. But now we see, as an awful revelation, that we are *all* called to be saints—not good necessarily, or pious or devout, but saints in the sense of just loving each other. In such exercises as these, we realize that we want to do that and that we can.

The workshops often close with a practice that is corollary to the earlier death meditation, in which we recognized that the person we meet may die in a nuclear war. Look at the next person you see. It may be someone else (lover, child, co-worker, mail carrier), or your own face in the mirror. Regard him or her with the recognition that

This person before me may be instrumental in saving us from nuclear war. In this person are gifts for the healing of our planet. Here are powers that can resound to the happiness of all beings.

RELATED READINGS

Lifton, Robert J. *The Broken Connection.* New York: Simon & Schuster, 1979. The most extensive study to date of the psychological impact of the nuclear threat.

Macy, Joanna R. *Despairwork.* Philadelphia: New Society Publishers, 1982.

_____. *Dharma and Development.* West Hartford, Conn.: Kumarian Press, 1983. An account of the role of Buddhism in the Sarvodaya Movement for village self-help in Sri Lanka.

_____. *Despair and Personal Power in the Nuclear Age.* Philadelphia: New Society Publishers, 1983.

SOURCES FOR THE MEDITATIONAL PRACTICES:

Background on the Death Meditation and Learning to See (the Brahmaviharas) can be found in Buddhaghosa's *Visuddhimagga* (Nanamoli, trans., *Path of Purification* [Colombo: Semage, 1956]); in Edward Conze's *Buddhist Meditation* (Bolinas, Calif.: Four Seasons Foundation, 1973) and in Macy's *Dharma and Development.*

"Breathing Through" is adapted from Tibetan exercises for the development of *bodhicitta,* the motivation to devote oneself to the liberation of all beings. A written account of some of them can be found in Lama Dhargyey's *Tibetan Tradition of Mental Development,* Library of Tibetan Archives (Dharamsala, 1974).

The Great Ball of Merit is derived from chapter 6 of *The Perfection of Wisdom in Eight Thousand Verses,* edited and translated by Edward Conze (London: Allen & Unwin, 1956).

8. Hindsight Prayer and Compassion

JOHN HAUGHEY, S.J.

For a volume that is concerned with social compassion, I have an odd recommendation to make: The most compassionate thing you can do is to "know thyself." Compassion is necessary where there are victims. But to the extent that we do not know ourselves, we are continually making victims or inciting tensions that require others to be compassionate to those we have hurt, however unconsciously. By greater self-knowledge we can reduce or eliminate the social tension, hostility, or violence we ourselves are causing. Compassion can be a "Band-Aid" activity; self-knowledge can sometimes get to the source of the infection.

A single example should suffice to make the point. It comes from a university department that I know of that on the surface is running smoothly. All the members speak to one another with civility and respect. That respect is shown more by the distance that they have learned to keep from one another than by their degree of engagement. We will zoom our lens in on one of the members of the department. The relationship between social compassion and self-knowledge came to the fore in something that happened to him recently.

He had a dream that awakened in his consciousness something that he had put out of his mind, an incident that had happened several years ago. The dream was his subconscious informing his conscious mind to attend to something that he had neglected. It was easy for him to recognize the actual incident that the dream hinted at; it involved his relationship with a colleague who had embarrassed him in a public session. Once he recalled the incident as vividly as he could, it didn't take long for his embarrassment and resentment to well up anew. He was then faced with a choice: either fume all over again about this or bring the matter before the Lord so that his emotions could be dealt with in the presence of God. With some reluctance and only slowly, he chose the latter course. This newly remembered, longforgotten datum of consciousness became the subject matter of his prayer.

He followed more or less the structure of the Examen that he had learned from the Spiritual Exercises of Saint Ignatius. Since that particular exercise is an exercise of prayer, it begins with an attempt to place oneself in God's presence.[1] If this is not done, the rest of the exercise is more likely to be an exercise in introspection and rekindling of anger than prayer. A fresh awareness of God's presence should prompt a sense of gratitude for his favors. This is immediately followed by a prayer of petition: to know what one's sins are and to be given to know what to do in order to be rid of those sins.[2]

In this case, the sincerity of his petition forced him to try to go deeper than the gall that the incident awakened in him. He sought to find out what in his own behavior incited his colleague to his behavior. Before long he came to see how some of his own behavior was, in fact, threatening his colleague; he himself helped create the situation wherein he was attacked. He also became aware that he had seldom recognized his colleague for his research efforts. He also began to suspect that he had made his colleague the scapegoat for prior resentments and skirmishes with other people. Finally, he became aware that he had never shared his own uncertainties with his colleague and, in fact, refused to make himself vulnerable to him at all. As a result, his colleague misread him as more secure than he actually felt, as imperious, even.

The effect of all of this retrieval and examination was the beginning of a realization that he himself was at least half the problem, if not more. Rather than being aware of this or admitting this before, he had begun to encase the other person with the mud that his judgments had flung on him over the course of time. That mud quickly hardened into an impasse. "He is this way and I refuse to accept his way of being, thinking, performing, judging, and acting," he had said, in effect. "I don't accept him as he is. The impasse will break once he changes, and that's all there is to the matter."

Part of the prayer method he employed was to place himself in the several scenes that burned most deeply in his memory about their relationship. The contemplation method of the Spiritual Exercises would have the one praying "see the characters, hear their words, and see their actions."[3] By this combination of Ignatian contemplation and Ignatian Examen, the past episodes became present. He began to dialogue with the Lord about his part in the disharmony between himself and his colleague.

The next point recommended by Ignatius in the Examen process is forgiveness. Ignatius recommends that we seek to be forgiven by God, whom we have offended by our behavior. The offended colleague found himself loath to do this, and it took him several days before he wanted to ask God to forgive him. At present he is doing so only superficially. But at least he knows that he must begin to take action, this one and others, to break the impasse.

The issue of forgiveness doesn't stop simply with being reconciled with God. There must also be an attempt at reconciliation between the two parties. A mere vertical clearing of his own conscience or an intramental reconciliation of himself with God would be insufficient, since several people (in fact a whole department of people) are affected by this situation. There is also the healing of his own memories, not only of these moments of hurt and hostility, but also of scenes still to be retrieved that antedate the relationship in question. What remains finally to be done is something that Ignatius calls a purpose of amendment, whereby one shows oneself sincere in receiving the grace that God gives in order to effect a change.

So much for the process. Notice it was not automatic with the person cited in this example. In fact, the Examen of consciousness only began a process of reconciliation, which presumably will take a fairly long time, since habits of estrangement and antagonism have become part of the behavior of both parties.

I cite this example in order to make my point concrete. The most compassionate thing anyone can do is deal with the situations that are before them. Both parties in my example spend much of their energy being compassionate toward others. What the offended colleague learned in his prayer recalled for him the relevance of Isaiah 58:6f.: "This . . . is the fasting that I wish:

releasing those bound unjustly, untying the thongs of the yoke; setting free the oppressed, breaking every yoke . . . remove from your midst oppression, false accusation and malicious speech."

There are two prayer forms that can greatly assist a person in achieving self-knowledge. Both require hindsight. Both have their origin, for me at least, in the Spiritual Exercises of Ignatius Loyola, although I will indicate how they can be adapted.

All prayer involves a pray-er, God, and some content or subject matter. The subject matter for the first practice of prayer that I am recommending here will come from something that I retrieve from my immediate past, something that has already happened in my consciousness. It has a retrospective quality to it, at least initially.

The particular item to be retrieved is some matter that has occupied my attention. It could be a relationship, a worry, a task, an interest, something I have been thinking about or studying, a conversation, even a stray remark. If it is not brought forward into my consciousness again, it will have already "done its thing" to me. One of the purposes of this prayer exercise is for me to re-experience my experiencing, understanding, judging, and choosing in order to confirm or disown what I have experienced. There is a need to differentiate from my own consciousness the objects my intending focuses on in order to more freely choose what I am doing with my life.[4]

But, one could rightly object, the data of consciousness are many, and the objects focusing our intentionality are many. The more important ones are those suffused with a significant degree of affectivity, positive or negative, according to Ignatius, and behind this contention is a world view.

The world view of Ignatius of Loyola can be caught in several expressions: the call of Christ the King, companionship, and the service of the King. Because of the difficulty he himself experienced in trying to sort out the call of the Lord to him, Ignatius mapped out a series of directions for those who, with like ardor, sought to hear and follow their call. These directions, succinctly encapsuled in the Spiritual Exercises, are ingenious as much for the directions that they do not give as for those they do give.

The directions they give are Ignatius' attempt to elaborate a general scheme for locating God's call, both the call to vocation itself and its daily particulars. Once the directional or vocational call has been discovered, Ignatius would place the Examen of conscience at the top of the list of practices necessary to continue to discern the particularities of God's call in Christ. If one should find on a given day that there is no time for formal prayer because of the press of the activities, one was not to omit the Examen, so greatly did Ignatius value such an exercise. In fact, in his own life the practice became so habitual that he examined himself seven or eight times a day, he told his biographer.[5]

Part of Ignatius' interest in the Examen was purity of intention, that is, that all might be done by the follower of Christ for the glory of God. Ignatius was aware that any good work or undertaking could begin with the best of intentions and imperceptibly be twisted into something serving one's own ends rather than God's glory. Equally possible was a work that was not good from the beginning even though it purported to be God's will. One could expend a lifetime of energy on it without detecting the evil source of the attraction. Thus purity was only one reason for the Examen; the other was so that one would be continually open to the ongoing call of Christ within one's particular vocational choice. To do this, Ignatius encourages us to become masters of the discernment of spirits moving in our hearts.

Ignatius saw everyone, not only those who would live a holy life, as terrain on which a battle was fought. But the battle had only a slight impact on each person's consciousness, so it was imperative that the consciousness become more sensitive to the influences working on it. The plaintiffs of the dispute lie both within the personality and beyond it. Those within the personality Jung would eventually name the ego and the self. But for Ignatius the plaintiffs were Christ and Satan or the good and the evil spirit. He did not theorize about them but provided two major assists to the tradition of spiritual discernment that the church has since appropriated.

One is a simple description of the strategy of these two would-be conquerors of the person. In his meditation of the Two Standards, Ignatius suggests that Satan lures us in three successive ways into confusion about ourselves. The first lure is to value ourselves as human beings according to the value of our possessions.[6] Once we are confused in this way, Satan takes us to the next step, which is to seek social confirmation of our initial mistake about ourselves and our value. The third step is to bring us to the fallacious understanding that we are entirely our own persons, that we are autonomous.

Jesus' strategy, by contrast, is not obscure but stands forth for all who would seek to hear it. He first of all invites us to disengage the sense of ourselves from what we have or might acquire.[7] Ignatius sees Christ then attracting us to a self-affirmation before God and others without having to be esteemed by others for what we have or what position we occupy or what honors we have attained. Thirdly, Christ attracts us to a self-perception of heteronomy and companionship. Or, as Paul would say, "For, to me, life means Christ" (Phil. 1:21).

The Examen prayer, for Ignatius, seeks to enable us to become sensitive to which strategy is influencing us or attempting to influence us. Seeing more clearly whose strategy we are being lured by through the objects filling our consciousness, we can more fully choose to come under the standard of Christ. The Examen is, therefore, an exercise in "the discernment of spirits."[8]

By developing the practice of reviewing some of the significant attractions or conflicts we have experienced since our last review, we can grow more aware of the sources of these feelings, thoughts, and impulses. The Examen and the discernment of spirits, therefore, presumes that God can be known and his call heard within the swirl of the ordinary secular happenings of one's day. An Examen, furthermore, is a prayer that pays particular attention to the feelings suffusing these small events in order to see where they are coming from and where they are leading. In this way one learns to differentiate the authentic from the inauthentic inspirations and thus choose more freely between them. Something more needs to be said about these affectivities.

Ignatius' experience led him to this rule of thumb: "In souls that are progressing to greater perfection, the action of the good angel is delicate, gentle, delightful. It may be compared to a drop of water penetrating a sponge."[9] In such persons the contrary action of the evil spirit is "violent, noisy, and disturbing. It may be compared to a drop of water falling on a stone."[10] By contrast, for a person whose heart is hardened to God, there is a natural attraction toward the coarse and sensual. Hence, when God is seeking to draw such a person from this hardness of heart, the action of the Spirit is one that jars or rattles.

It would be good, of course, if it were as simple as that. One problem is that only some of our positive and negative affectivity has "the spirits" as its source. The other problem is that "the evil one" never tempts with coarseness the person who is earnestly striving to be in union with God. Discernment is needed, first of all, to perceive whether discernment of spirits is needed. It is not necessary when it is obvious what it is that is moving the person.

For example, when a person is obviously moved toward the crude, discernment is not necessary but simple steadfastness in the face of temptation. Discernment *is* necessary when there is an impulse toward an apparent good that does not come from God but is not seen as such. Ignatius' term "the evil one" is a summary symbol for the many forces that blur, distract, confuse, our ability to detect the particular ways God is attracting us to union in him and to mission. Hence, discernment is concerned to help one avoid expending energy in what is not an attraction of God.

Specifically, Examen is seeking to detect the particulars of the call that Christ has for the person. Discernment is not concerned with the choice of good over evil but with the particular good among many goods that God would have the person undertake. The prayer of the Examen is superfluous or foolish to a person who thinks that the range of good he or she should do can be confined to or exhausted by conformity to general norms. The prayer of the Examen presupposes that the one who has been invited to follow the Lord will be invited to behavior that can neither be known ahead of time nor universalized. Since the impetus behind the invitation is extended by the Son out of love, it is only the Spirit of love that can accurately hear the voice of the beloved. Although it is true that the call of Christ is to a way of life that can be both taught and known, nevertheless, that way can only be known in general. It is not known in its particulars; the unfolding, concrete aspects of one's call cannot be known ahead of time or by anyone other than the one being invited.

In brief, the Ignatian Examen is an exercise in nonobjective perception; not in the sense that it is subjective but in the sense that it is radically interpersonal. It is a needless exercise for those who do not know themselves or who have not detected in the depths of themselves the presence of God loving them and calling them to union with and service of him. But the concrete imperative that each is seeking to perceive is situated in a unique history of invitation heard, commitment made, and powers bestowed.[11]

Ignatius lists the negative affects as anxieties, sadness, confusion, restlessness, or listlessness about the things of God and an inclination toward things that are crude.[12] Positive feelings, by contrast, are joy in the performance of our tasks, love of our associates, peace, patience, faith, hope, trust, courage, and in general an attraction for the things of God. Of much less importance are the ideas we have or the projects we are pursuing. There are, of course, times when the matter for the Examen can be more easily located in our thoughts or choices, plans or projects, than in our affectivity, but even then, Ignatius would have us seek in prayer to detect the affect with which they are clothed.

As prayer, the Examen is an exercise in discerning the fit or lack of it between the concrete self as it has acted, chosen, and felt and the sensed presence of Jesus. Through the Examen we lie open to being corrected or confirmed in what we have taken to be Christ's will for us and word to us. The Examen is concerned to bring us beyond our own devisings to a deeper sense of call and a a deeper sense of commitment to following Christ. Using this prayer over time, Ignatius was convinced, people could develop a sixth sense with which to detect "the voice of the bridegroom of their soul."

The limitations of Ignatius' directions for hindsight prayer are several. For one thing, we have come to understand considerably more about the psyche and its affectivity than Ignatius could have known. The explosion of understanding that has come about, especially since Freud and the development of the psychotherapeutic processes, make Ignatius' sixteenth-century setting appear at times somewhat quaint. To make it complete, a twentieth-century Christian would have to take Ignatius' contribution through the critical mediation of these recent findings. Notwithstanding its limitations, Ignatius' orientation continues to be invaluable to many, and since the psychotherapeutic sciences are not themselves without considerable confusion, these sources of understanding can complement each other.

The other limitation of the Examen is its frequent reduction to an exercise in moralistic scouring or introspection. The emphasis on consciousness in recent times has happily changed the exercise, moving away from an emphasis on conscience.[13] Introspection, furthermore, is always a danger with any form of prayer. Care with the beginnings of the Examen, especially the "placing of oneself in the presence of God," should help to reduce the chances of this happening.[14]

Whereas the Examen prayer can examine negative and positive affectivity and their spiritual implications, there is another Ignatian prayer form that has more to do with our positive feelings. In fact, Ignatius would see Christians capable of generating a greater degree of spiritual energy from this kind of prayer. Like the Examen, this prayer form is also hindsight prayer, because it goes back over our experience and ferrets out its overlooked significance, its love meaning. The locus for this prayer form is also the Spiritual Exercises; it is poorly entitled "The Contemplation to Attain the Love of God." I say "poorly entitled" because it is not an attempt to attain the love of God; it is an exercise that gets us in touch with God loving us. A successful use of this form of prayer should enable us to become centers of compassion toward others because we will have arrived at a continuing consciousness of the compassion of God for us.

Although this prayer form is the final exercise in the Spiritual Exercises of Saint Ignatius and is much more fruitfully used by those who have undergone the discipline of those exercises, the prayer form can also be useful for others. The fruit that derives from the use of such a prayer form would be slower in ripening without the discipline of the exercises, but it could be forthcoming nonetheless. The purpose of the prayer is very simple: to receive an intimate knowledge of the things that affect one's life as not discrete happenings but gifts from one source. A person who grows in the use of such a prayer form comes to see the myriad of ordinary things as so many gifts by which God is particularizing his love. The prayer form does not seek to arrive at some kind of metaphysical vision of the origin of all created reality; it seeks, rather, to recognize the interpersonal origin of all that touches one's life.

Like all prayer, this prayer form begins not with an idea but with a sense of the need for God's power to change blindness into recognition so that mutuality between God and the person can be evoked. The prayer begins, therefore, imploring "an intimate knowledge of the many blessings received." Ignatius himself attained to an almost continual awareness of "God giving himself to me" in all of the created realities that surrounded his life. The recognition evokes a response in kind, a love response, a response from one's heart. God's compassion, showered upon the one who recognizes God's activity, becomes compassion for all who are affected by the life of the one who has been given this recognition. "Be compassionate, as your Father is compassionate . . . give . . . good measure pressed down, shaken together, running over" (Luke 6:36–38).

Before elaborating the structure of this prayer, Ignatius seeks our assent on two presuppositions. The first is that love is shown in deeds. Words of love may or may not be love, but when love is shown in deeds, then love is indeed being shown. This is Ignatius' insight into both the character of love and the character of God. Interiority always translates into history. The Spirit can give us a vision of our history as the deeds of God's love, and what is whispered in the dark of the heart is propelled forth into actions that respond to the love the heart has perceived operating on our behalf. *Via* this ongoing perception we can live within the positive affectivity of consolation.

But this sense of consolation or of God's acting on our behalf is only half of the story. The consciousness leads to a deed by way of response to the love. Love is evoked by love. Once God's love activity is recognized, mutuality begins to develop. Depending upon the depth of recognition, the mutuality begins to take the form of "a mutual sharing of one's goods." "The lover gives and shares with the beloved what he possesses, or something of that which he has or is able to give; and vice versa, the beloved shares with the lover."[15] "Hence, if one has knowledge he shares it with the one who does not possess it; and so also if one has honors, or riches. Thus one always gives to the other." These are Ignatius' observations about the character of all love, deriving, of course, from his experience of human love. If we assent to this characterization, the subsequent prayer form is simple and beautiful.

I should also say that this prayer form presumes that we are open to a high level of affective response to a sense of God's presence and have a deep yearning for union with God. And this exercise comes at the end of our gradual identification with our Lord as friend and beloved, after strenuous exercises to come to freedom about the disposition of ourselves. Hence, the prayer form presumes that we using it have achieved a degree of personal freedom from disordered affectivity whereby we can dispose our lives at the behest of God's call.

The prayer can proceed in four different though related ways. The first way is to recall the particulars of our life. The particulars can either be from the created order or from the order of redemption, although the distinction becomes less and less clear the more we become one with the beloved. We can revert to our most recent involvements or our immediate past, or we can sweep back through our whole graced history. Either way, we seek to see God particularizing his love, his favoring of us, through each of these particulars. Once we locate the particulars, the reflection is done "with great affection." Depending on the depth to which our affectivity has been touched, we can exclaim, like Ignatius, "How much God our Lord has done for me, and how much he has given me of what he possesses, and finally how much he desires to give Himself to me."

But the matter does not stay simply in the savoring or the tasting or the attending to the way in which we have been favored by God. Ignatius, employing the first two presuppositions about the character of love, then has us seek to reciprocate from the depths of our own evoked feelings with whatever love deeds we are prompted to offer to God. We must, therefore, be aware of what we possess in order to bring it forward and make a gift of it to the beloved. Some things are more extricable than others. Ignatius disposes of his own liberty, his memory, his understanding, in a manner of speaking.[16]

There are three different ways of doing this basic form of

prayer. The first focuses on everything about ourselves and begins to see every aspect as gift. Through this appreciation of ourselves, the floodgates of thanks and praise to God are opened. We can be moved "by great feeling" to see ourselves as extraordinary, as indwelt by God or as receiving our whole reality from him; we can see ourselves as God's temple or as made in the image and likeness of God. Or we can see the particulars of our own body or mind or spirit and come to an awareness of the extraordinary thing that it is to be.

The appreciation of ourselves and of ourselves as the sum total of all of God's gifts lovingly centered in our person evokes a desire to respond with the very personhood that is newly appreciated; hence the desire to put at the service of God every talent and feature of my gifted personhood. "Since all is thine, dispose of it wholly according to thy will. Give me only thy love and thy grace; that is enough for me." Love is not onesided, it is interpersonal.

There is a circle between what has exited from God to us because to him we now return all the ways in which we find ourselves gifted. All of our ordinary, pedestrian activity can take on a new quality; it can be a way of completing the circle of love that has pierced our heart, making our activity contemplative in its spirit, purpose, and character. The habit of hindsight prayer can develop enormous spiritual bouyancy. Activity can flow from heartfelt, interior recognition of God continually gifting.[17]

A slightly different focus that this prayer form can take is also suggested by Ignatius, in his recommendation that we focus on whatever created things have touched our lives today, for example, "the elements, plants, fruit, cattle." We can begin to see these particular things in a new perspective. We can see God at work in and through them: "Conducting himself as one who works for me in all creatures." This vision makes sacred the most pedestrian of things. Infinite love is continually becoming very finite deeds on our behalf in order that the very finite deeds that we do might be directed toward the infinite love of God. Our smallest labors and actions, in other words, have a new potential for being ways of loving God. Our work life can, therefore, lose its secular nature; the ordinary can be made sacred.

As a final way to do this form of hindsight prayer Ignatius

suggests employing the faculty of imagination rather than memory. It focuses on qualities or virtues or abilities that we and others have. So, for example, the ability to be just, compassionate, merciful, courteous, or intelligent: We do not dwell on these powers for long in a static way but begin to see them flowing out through people, ourselves and others. Rather than follow them to their terminal point, we go back to their origins. All human instances of such qualities are signs of their origin. The justice of God is manifested in justice in the world, the compassion of God is manifested through human compassion, and so on. All beautiful human qualities "descend from above as the rays of light descend from the sun, and as the waters flow from their fountains."[18]

I like to see Jesus himself as the embodiment of this form of prayer. He was the perfect response to all the *creata* that surrounded him. He loved all things in his Father, and he saw his Father working in all things. He loved things each in themselves, but he also loved each thing in his Father. He became in his own person a center of enormous positive affectivity. Hence, he could radiate to others the compassion of God that he had internalized. His Father's compassion extended toward him in innumerable finite, particular ways. He schooled himself to see all of those ways; hence he became like the One who loved him, "perfect as your heavenly Father is perfect" (Matt. 5:48). He became the compassion of God.

NOTES

1. *The Spiritual Exercises of St. Ignatius,* ed. Louis Puhl, S.J. (Chicago: Loyola University Press, 1951), no. 43.
2. Ibid.
3. Ibid., nos. 106–108.
4. Bernard Lonergan, *Method in Theology* (New York: Herder & Herder, 1972), pp. 14–15.
5. Joseph de Guibert, *The Jesuits: Their Spiritual Doctrine and Practice* (Chicago: Loyola University Press, 1964), pp. 39–40, 66–68.
6. *Spiritual Exercises,* no. 142. The instruments of Satan are being told "to tempt [people] to covet riches."
7. Ibid., no. 146. The followers of Jesus are instructed to attract potential followers of Jesus "to the highest spiritual poverty, and . . . if he chooses them for it, even to actual poverty."

8. Ibid., no. 313–336.
9. Ibid., no. 335.
10. Ibid., no. 335.
11. Karl Rahner, "The Logic of Concrete Individual Knowledge in Ignatius Loyola," in *The Dynamic Element in the Church* (New York: Herder & Herder, 1964), pp. 84–156.
12. *Spiritual Exercises*, no. 317.
13. George Aschenbrenner, "Consciousness Examen," *Review for Religious* 31 (1972), pp. 14–21.
14. *Spiritual Exercises*, no. 46.
15. Ibid., no. 231.
16. Ibid., no. 234.
17. Michael Buckley, "The Contemplation to Attain Love," *The Way* (Supplement no. 24), pp. 92–104. This is the best introduction to the "contemplatio" form of prayer I know of.
18. *Spiritual Exercises*, no. 237.

9. Seeking a Suitable Spirituality in a Sect Becoming Catholic

E. GLENN HINSON

As I examine in this chapter the possibilities and constrictions of spiritual resources in the Southern Baptist situation and its larger context of historical and contemporary spiritualities, I hope readers will be able to make their own application to their particular denomination's life. Each of us needs to be willing to own up honestly to the shortcomings and needs, as well as strengths, of our faith communion if we are to respond to our critical world situation with adequate spiritual depth.

A plethora of problems plagues Southern Baptist spirituality in this apocalyptic era. As if facing apocalypse with these deficiencies were not enough in and of itself, this seventeenth-century offspring of the Radical Reformation is rapidly rumbling into the catholic phase of its history. Numerically dominant in virtually every county south of the Mason-Dixon line and east of Texas, these latter-day Nonconformists have taken on the features of an established church without compensating for the loss of sectarian spontaneity and community consciousness with catholic discipline, structure, and tradition. The net effect of this intricate combination of factors is near-complete unpreparedness for a time of stress and frantic flailing in search of a suitable spirituality.

ILL-EQUIPPED FOR APOCALYPSE

Inheritors of a spirituality shaped largely by way of reaction against abuses in the exercise of authority over the lives of individuals, Southern Baptists have tended to place responsibility heavily on the shoulders of the individual and to eschew means for the cultivation of piety. They have viewed formation as wholly repugnant to the liberty of the believer. More heavily influenced by American revivalism than most denominations, they have put the accent on the front end of the religious pilgrimage and neglected the growth process. Indeed, the emphasis on grace as unmerited forgiveness and the fear of legalism that they share with other Protestants have resulted often in the watering down of the divine demand to the point of irresponsibility. This is not to say there have been no Southern Baptist saints. There have been. But such saints have come about more by divine "accident," or perhaps "the double search" of God and the individual, than by corporate design.

To begin this assessment with the *goal* of spirituality (surely the main basis for any critique), Southern Baptist acceptance of the Protestant emphasis on grace as God's unmerited favor in forgiveness, exhibited especially in a forensic concept of justification rather than as the Holy Spirit poured into our hearts and working effectually within to create righteousness, has had a leveling effect on spirituality, encouraging what Bonhoeffer called "cheap grace." "Jesus paid it all. All to Him I owe. Sin had left its crimson stain. He washed it white as snow," we Southern Baptists love to sing. To think there may be more that we are obliged to do would militate against this understanding of "grace that is greater than all our sins" and that leaves nothing more to be done to put ourselves right with God. "Once saved, always saved," runs a popular Southern Baptist saying. Development of means of growth might lead to a "works righteousness," against which the Apostle Paul spoke so vigorously.

If this concept of grace has made the rough places plain, Protestant repudiation of levels of piety and correlate emphasis on the priesthood of all believers, admirable as they may have been as a goal, have resulted in the discarding of most of the models of piety that have guided Christians through the centuries. Like their early forebears, Southern Baptists have used up quite a bit of ink noting that Paul labeled all Christians "saints" and repudiating the idea of a "favored few." They have viewed with horror the calendar of saints' days, prayer through the saints and Mary, the monastic vocation, and, in general, the whole concept of "holy persons." If the faithful selected models, they should choose biblical models. Yet many Southern Baptists have undercut any expectation of matching the level of piety exhibited in the Bible by putting persons of the biblical era in an altogether separate category of those living in an era wherein the Holy Spirit inspired saints in a way no longer to be expected. According to Protestant Dispensationalism, so influential in the Southern Baptist sphere, the Holy Spirit all but ceased to function entirely after inspiring the last New Testament writing, perhaps holding out on its deathbed until the canon was finalized about A.D. 400.

If the *goal* of spirituality has suffered diminishment, so have the *means* offered for achieving the goal. Following in the footsteps of the Puritans, Southern Baptists have substituted Scriptures, sermon, and prayer for statuary, icons, stained glass windows, relics, pilgrimages, saints' days, processions, lights, the sacraments, liturgies, singing, confessionals, and all the other paraphernalia of piety. They have retained two sacraments (scrupulously called "ordinances"), baptism and the Lord's Supper, but Scriptures and sermon have taken pride of place as the means through which they expect God to communicate his grace to the faithful.

Southern Baptist spirituality, it can be said without many qualifiers, has centered on the Bible, especially the New Testament. Corporate worship has revolved around reading and exposition of the Scriptures and prayer. Private devotion has focused on reading of the Scriptures and spontaneous prayer. Although Bible-centered piety has produced a Clarence Jordan and a Martin Luther King, Jr., here and there, the circumscribing of the means of grace has resulted in a certain impoverishment with respect to how individual believers discover and respond to grace at work within them. Until recent years, for instance, Southern Baptists have shied away from devotional classics, counting themselves people of one book, the Bible, and thus they have cut themselves off from the wisdom of centuries. Meanwhile, they have lost touch with the classical approach to Christian meditation on the Bible.

The sermon has taken and does take second place only to the

Scriptures as a means of grace, ranking far above sacraments in this regard. The Word of God, Southern Baptists assume, comes, above all, through Scriptures and sermon. If biblical, the sermon will reprove, rebuke, exhort, inspire, encourage, comfort, and direct the sinful saint. It can touch every aspect of life. Using the shotgun rather than the rifle approach, however, it has not substituted fully for the many aids to devotion that it replaced, particularly the more personalized and individualized assistance of spiritual counselors and directors. Southern Baptist piety, as a consequence, has depended on individual, personal proclivity and determination rather than corporate design.

The same problem has afflicted the Southern Baptist practice of prayer. Southern Baptists have talked about and exhorted to prayer, but they have deprived themselves of most of the art of praying and, more costly, virtually slammed the door shut on the main schools of prayer—the liturgy, great prayers of Christian history, and the contemplative tradition. Until recently, imitating their forefathers, they have repudiated the use even of the Lord's Prayer as an aid to teaching converts or children how to pray. If you want children to learn how, prescribed John Bunyan, tell them about the fires of hell, and they will know how. Bunyan, however, like the Reformers of the sixteenth century, knew how to pray because he was not far removed from the inheritance of a praying church. His twentieth-century heirs are not so close, and myriads have forgotten how to pray. Thus they are turning elsewhere to get some tutoring.

If Baptists, along with other Protestants, gained something of the cognitive dimension of religion in this shift from a liturgical/sacramental/confessional/contemplative to a biblical/sermonic piety, they also lost something in the way of affective and intuitive dimensions of piety, that is, in the cultivation of what Theodore Roszak calls "the powers of transcendence." They have touched the head more than the heart. As a result, they have had to fumble around to find media to make up for the loss. Music, eschewed by early Baptists, has been called on increasingly to fill the liturgical gap. The hymns of the faith come closer to the heart. Art and architecture and the calendar and other aids have made a comeback little by little. In the main, however, Southern Baptists have relied on religious fervor stirred up by fiery sermons in the fashion of frontier revivals to make up for the affective aid of the liturgy, the mass, and the complex system of the cure of souls put together over many centuries.

The ultimate test of spirituality, however, should rest neither in goal nor in means but in *effects*. What is the product? Already I have mentioned "rootlessness," "superficiality," "narrow social vision," and "confusion of ends and means." To these many would add "autonomism," or "selfish privatism." Southern Baptist spirituality, I am convinced, is producing too few saints and exercising too little encouragement to sanctification. It encourages compartmentalization—here religion and there the life of every day—and fails to sufficiently awaken the faithful to the experience of grace in the mundane and ordinary as well as in the "heights." It leaves too many adherents stunted in religious infancy.

OPTIONS OFFERED

Several options for correcting some of these deficiencies have been offered during the past two decades. Three merit special mention: secular spirituality, charismatic spirituality, and quasi-Eastern spirituality. Like other Protestants, Southern Baptists have sampled each in a limited way.

SECULAR SPIRITUALITY

Secular spirituality attempted to overcome the gap between sacred and secular, the Church and the world, the City of God and the secular city. Sparked by the musings of Dietrich Bonhoeffer in his *Letters and Papers from Prison,* in its extreme form it became "God is dead" theology. Since the latter is itself now dead, however, I will mention only the moderate interpretations and applications of Bonhoeffer's thought that evoked a search for what John A. T. Robinson called "worldly holiness."

As Bishop Robinson construed it, "worldly holiness" would involve discernment of the holy in the common, engagement rather than disengagement from the world, and a "nonreligious" understanding of prayer. Like Bonhoeffer, Robinson suggested that we look for "the 'beyond' *in the midst of our life"* and not "out there." Thus the Christian Eucharist and the liturgy should help to unite rather than to separate us from humankind. "The test of worship," the Bishop insisted, "is how far it makes us *more sensitive* to 'the beyond in our midst,' to the Christ in the hungry, the naked, the homeless and the prisoner." [1] Accordingly, prayer should result in engagement—"penetration through the world to God" rather than "withdrawal from the world to God." [2] Intercession would not mean to mention another to God so much as "to be *with* another" in the presence of God, "whether in silence or compassion or action." [3] In this way the Christian life will be a life of "the man for others," of "holy worldliness," of "sacred secularity." [4]

The secular theologians deserve due credit here. They chided us enough to lure us out of "smug sanctuaries" into the world, where "the action is," presumably God's action as well as human action. The problem with their proposal lay in its tendency to level all things to one level. Yes, God *is* in the factory, the mine, the office, or the shop as in the sanctuary. Humanly considered, however, what is to inform and guide our action if we do not withdraw from the life of every day and seek Wisdom for its own sake periodically? Or, as Merton put it in responding to Bishop Robinson, what will we have to offer the world that the world doesn't already have?

The point is made for us, I think, by some secular theologians themselves. Harvey Cox, for instance, experienced a major transition from *The Secular City* (1965), in which he hymned metropolis, to *The Feast of Fools* (1969), in which he lauded medieval fantasizing. Subsequently, he discovered the charismatic movement (*The Seduction of the Spirit*, 1973) and Eastern religion (*Turning East*, 1977). Similarly, Douglas Rhymes, in *Prayer in the Secular City* (1967), defined prayer as "involvement of service which will carry us into the fields of politics, economics, welfare, social work" and as "a matter of practice rather than profession." [5] Seven years later (1974), in *Through Prayer to Reality,* he had shifted to the classical mode, affirming not only the need to reflect on "the meaning and the reality which lie behind our earthly living in the world" [6] but to "become more conscious of my true self, live more in accord with the nature of my true being, participate more in the divine nature." [7] Prayer, he now explained, is "all those times of living when one is practicing recollection, concentration, and the capacity of intuitive looking into the reality of all life."[8] Rhymes confessed too the value of the traditional stages of prayer—purgation, illumination, darkness, and union—for interpreting his own experience and the valve of the Bible as an aid in meditation.

CHARISMATIC SPIRITUALITY

Emerging during the 1950s, the neo-Pentecostal or charismatic movement within the mainline Protestant and Roman Catholic churches trumpeted a return to experiental religion, a search for "heart religion" to replace or to balance the prevalent "head religion" of American culture. Whereas the earlier Pentecostal movement of the late nineteenth and early twentieth centuries enlisted blue-collar, working-class people, this one captured the imagination of white-collar, well-educated, and culturally privileged people, the university crowd, testimony to the wearing effects of spreading secularity and of "the single vision" even in the religious sphere. The prevailing Protestant spirituality simply failed to satisfy.

Morton Kelsey is a leading savant of the charismatic movement. His theology of experience seems to me not yet to have received the attention it merits among academicans, but it has gotten enough hearing from laypeople to turn most theologians green with envy. Applying the insights of Jungian psychology, Kelsey has given clues for interpreting Christian experience in light of traditional Christian categories. On behalf of the charismatic movement, he is waging a battle for a more holistic approach to religion, one that will take into account the full range of "encounter with God." The idea of the supernatural has regained here some of its lost significance.

The charismatic movement deserves some accolades. To parody ecumenists, this movement may be the "great new fact of our time." Growing rapidly during the sixties and seventies, it has met religious needs neglected by formalistic and rationalistic public worship and gotten people excited again about faith. For many, who conceived this revival in too narrow terms, it fell short in much the same way earlier evangelical revivals did. It momentarily gratified a craving for experience, usually associated with speaking in tongues, but failed to sustain a growth process.

The "new birth" of a lot of "reborn" Christians thus died aborning. Morton Kelsey's numerous practical treatises on prayer, meditation, journal keeping, interpretation of dreams, Christian education, and other aspects of spiritual formation have filled a major need. Yet even his writings reflect some imbalances characteristic of this movement in general. Zeal to do battle for heart religion leads him to some neglect of head religion and social concern. Perhaps reformers have to go to extremes to make their case, but the two great commandments call for a better balance: They direct us to love God with all our heart, soul, mind, and strength and our neighbors as ourselves.[9]

QUASI-EASTERN SPIRITUALITY

One other trend in this period requires mention: the fascination Eastern spirituality holds for Protestants, particularly the youth. An intensive Gallup survey of the greater Dayton, Ohio, area revealed that 31 percent of the young people polled, far more than older people, had flirted with a host of religious movements and cults, including Eastern religions, Transcendental Meditation, and a variety of quasi-Oriental cults, despite the fact that 75 percent said they believed Jesus Christ is the Son of God. These same youths placed spiritual nourishment at the top of their list of goals and faulted the organized churches for neglecting it in their programs.[10] Mysticism and Eastern religions exert a powerful attraction over college youth in particular.[11] Robert Wuthnow concluded in a Pacific basin study of *Experimentation in American Religion* that four conditions in combination explained the success of Zen, TM, and yoga groups: exposure to new ideas; legitimation by the cultural milieu; opportunity for people to experiment; and motivation, the search for meaning, job or other pressures, personal problems, and so forth.[12]

The long-range effect of the encounter with Eastern spirituality cannot be established at this early date. Already, however, encounter with the East has heightened Christian concern for experience of the transcendent and either supplied new methods of meditation or goaded Christians to dig into their own dusty archives to recover long-discarded Christian methods.[13] Whatever their impact, nevertheless, I share Harvey Cox's suspicion[14] that the neo-Oriental cults will remain "far more 'neo' than 'Oriental,' " simply because Westerners will fail to assimilate them in depth. Christians will do better by letting the engagement with the East sprinkle their own experience than by taking the full plunge. Few, at any rate, will possess Thomas Merton's remarkable gift for tuning in on the wave length of Easterners sufficiently to be able to say, "I intend to become as good a Buddhist as I can."[15]

WHICH WAY DO WE TURN?

The question that now presses is in what direction do we turn? secular? charismatic? Eastern/mystical? or some other?

All of these, I would conclude, have made and can make significant contributions to the reformation of Southern Baptist spirituality. Secular theology must be heard for its summons to "worldly holiness," the charismatic movement for its wholesome accentuation of experience, and the spiritual *Drang nach Osten* for its challenge to the Western "single vision" and overreliance on what Merton characterized as pursuit of "external means to external ends." Granting full credit to each of these, however, it is doubtful whether any of them points in the proper direction, for none in itself solves the larger problem of Protestant spirituality.

We are fortunate that the present ecumenical climate not only makes it possible for us but even compels us to consider anew our understanding of the way in which we appropriate or experience the grace of God that transforms, renews, and directs our lives. If Southern Baptists are to throw off the straitjacket that the Reformers wrapped around their spirituality in the sixteenth century, they will have to recognize that grace means not merely "unmerited favor" but also "divine presence, love, and power" and that this grace ensures not only a declaration of acquittal of the sinner but also an enhancement of natural capabilities to grow in a personal way in one's relationship with God. More basically perhaps, they will also have to acknowledge that the experience of grace may occur not merely through individual but also through corporate channels.

When I challenge these assumptions, I realize I am dealing with matters that are not peripheral but central to the Protestant Reformation. By doing so, I in no way intend to deny that the Reformers were making a legitimate point. I'm acknowledging, rather, that they, in an excess of zeal to make their point, went too far and thus impaired Protestant spirituality. The most wholesome thing we can do for our spirituality, therefore, is to get it plugged back into the catholic tradition in order to draw again from its abundant waters. Thomas Merton has taught all of us here. He has shown that a tradition-anchored person can be fresh and relevant, indeed, that without tradition we run the greatest risk of irrelevancy in simply trying out the latest devotional fads. Merton drew his message of contemplation from the vast contemplative tradition running from the Old Testament via the New Testament to the Middle Ages and his own day. The farther he extended his pipeline outward toward the world of action, the more he sought solitude and the deeper he drilled into the contemplative tradition. Despite his fascination for such things as Zen Buddhism, he sifted everything through a catholic sieve constructed in his earlier years at the Trappist monastery at Gethsemani.

Back to the mainstream, then! If my own experience is typical, however, none of us can ignore or abandon our own tradition and plunge headlong into the Christian mainstream, as I once thought possible. We had best wade back through our own stream, even if it is but a trickle, and meet the larger stream where ours joins it. Each of our traditions, after all, possesses something that belongs to the very essence of the Christian tradition, as a branch draws sap from a tree, else it would have dried up long ago. The trick is to grasp the *essence* of our tradition, its *raison d'être*, so firmly that we will not fear letting go of the external and conventional features. When we have done that, then we will find ourselves at home in the mainstream as well.

When we get back to the mainstream, what then? Here I must speak chiefly as an heir of the Radical Reformation, which represented the opposite end of the spectrum from the medieval church. Ultimately, all of us have the same goal—obedience to

God, or in the words of the two great commandments, to "love God with all our heart, soul, mind, and strength" and to "love our neighbor as ourselves" (Mark 12:30–31). With my forebears, I still insist that such obedience and love must be voluntary, or they will not represent obedience at all. Coercion does not and cannot make saints. God's gracious love alone, his Spirit, freely responded to, makes saints. Unlike my forebears, however, I am willing to admit that the Spirit may work through the corporate—sacraments, priests, spiritual directors, the Church—as well as through the individual experience. Actually, my forebears *experienced* the Spirit corporately, even though in their beleaguered state they were reluctant to admit it and quick to deny it when they spoke of sacraments and priests. Today I do not feel the pressure they did to define their existence in terms of an experience other than the Roman Catholic or Anglican. Thus I can appreciate sacramental spirituality, spiritual direction, and the ascetic or contemplative tràdition in ways they could not.

However, I must go on to point out what my own tradition, the Free Church tradition, imposes upon me. Personal ecumania notwithstanding, I will sift all I find in the mainstream through a voluntarist sieve, reshaping or casting aside those elements that appear coercive. Consider spiritual direction and formation, for which many Protestants are hungering. None of us, surely, can ignore the record of oppressive authoritarianism that the Roman Catholic church compiled for itself in the late Middle Ages and after. As a descendant of Radicals, my imagination still conjures up images of inquisitions, monastic prisons, torture chambers, hangings, burnings, and those other paraphernalia of misguided zeal to save souls, and I can't dissociate these completely from authoritarian approaches to spiritual guidance. A recent "Concilium" volume devoted to *Christian Obedience* indicates that many Roman Catholics share my reservations. Although they caution against the "autonomism" and "selfish privatism" into which Protestants have frequently lapsed, noted authors such as Edward Schillebeeckx want freedom within which the Spirit can work within the individual's life. No more high-handed and arbitrary direction, they insist. No more slavish obeisance to religious superiors or spiritual directors. Spiritual directors must pay full heed to the personality of the person receiving instruction and guidance.[16]

My personal existence within a sect becoming catholic heightens my wariness here. If you range denominations across a spectrum from voluntarist, in which the Spirit is believed to effect obedience through the individual will, to intentionalist or corporatist, in which the Spirit is believed to effect obedience through the Church's corporate will, at the beginning Baptists would have occupied the extreme voluntarist end, alongside Quakers, and Roman Catholics the extreme intentionalist end. That is far from the situation today. Since the Second Vatican Council, while Roman Catholics have been sliding across the scale toward the voluntarist end, Southern Baptists have zipped in the opposite direction, passing many Roman Catholics going the other way. Many, if they could, would impose a stereotyped spirituality on all Southern Baptists, an essentially cognitive one drawn from Fundamentalism. In tapping again into the mainstream of Christian spirituality, we should be vigilant lest we get swept away in dangerous eddies toward authoritarian rapids that we tried to flee at the Reformation.

What kind of spiritual direction do I think feasible? Obviously, whatever it is, it must be voluntarist, sought by the individual and not imposed from above. Tilden Edwards has pointed out helpfully that spiritual direction can be mutual rather than one-way, even if a "one-way" approach "*can* take place *within* a mutual-direction relationship."[17] Furthermore, numerous personal factors should be taken into account—age, sex, experience, personality, spiritual path, faith tradition, situation, and so forth—and the relationship established by a voluntary "covenant." Personally, I am inclined to favor small group direction rather than individual precisely because it elevates the voluntarist aspect. When students or others come to me seeking spiritual guidance, I usually suggest that they take the initiative to form a group with others who have a similar interest. When the group is formed, I emphasize the importance of working out a covenant with one another that all can accept. If anyone wants individual counsel, I am open to that, but I have a modest opinion of my own skills and gifts for spiritual direction, and I am quick to refer them to others in whom I have confidence. As to the dynamics of group direction, I strive to be a good listener and to encourage listening in the group as the best means for getting in touch with the grace of God at work within.

I'm confessing here a bit of foot-dragging for people of my own tradition vis-à-vis a powerful current trend toward uncritical imitation of ancient and medieval models of spirituality. Richard J. Foster, a bright young Quaker, for instance, has sounded a call to recover the spiritual disciplines of meditation, prayer, fasting, study, simplicity, solitude, submission, service, confession, worship, guidance, and celebration as the "door to liberation."[18] What I fear, despite his disclaimers and cautions, is that focus on disciplines will lapse into disciplines and get hung up there—tithing mint, dill, and cummin and neglecting the weightier matters of the law (Matt. 23:23), as has happened countless times in the past. Perhaps I'm too Protestant, or Augustinian, or Pauline, but I perceive our task as helping one another push open the doors and windows of our hearts to let God's love and light flood our inmost chambers, very much as my earliest forebears did. Stated another way, it is to help one another become conscious of the work of divine grace within, for it is this grace that must transform and nurture and perfect us in love.

GETTING IN TOUCH WITH GRACE AT WORK

How, then, do we become aware of and get in touch with the operation of grace? At the outset it would be well to remind ourselves that not everything depends on us; perhaps it would be more accurate to say that *not much* depends on us. As Rufus Jones has reminded us, there is a double search: We seek God, but, just as surely, he is unrelenting in his search for us. "God lies in wait for us . . .," said Meister Eckhart,[19] "with nothing so much as love." How to let God spring his surprise on us should be our chief concern.

CORPORATE EXPERIENCE

At the risk of sounding contradictory, I would begin with *corporate experience.* Most of us, whether Protestant, Catholic, or Orthodox, have tasted the love and the grace of God first through gathering with others in public worship or in fellowship with one another. Even John Bunyan, insistent as he was on *individual* experience, recounted the importance of both Anglican churches and the little congregation at Bedford that he later served as pastor. Overhearing some saintly women from the latter brought him to the brink of conversion. Interpreter's House in *Pilgrim's Progress* is, almost certainly, the Church.

Different people will have had varied experiences of "church." My own has ranged from small rural, large urban, and cosmopolitan European congregations representing many denominations to the oecumene of the World Council of Churches. Yet the longer I live and the more experiences I have, the more impressed I am with the wealth of love and grace that we must presuppose to account for these diverse families. The survival of a natural family in our age and circumstances requires a generous amount of love. How, then, can we fail to be quite overwhelmed by the love that binds together disparate and diverse people—male and female, black and white, young and old, wealthy and poor, educated and uneducated—into a church family? Does grace not operate more often in spite of than because of us?

The key question for us today is How will the churches carry out their midwifery and mothering more effectively? In asking it, we open up the immense problem of being the Church, living in the Spirit and letting grace flow through our lives as we continue Christ's ministry in and to the world. Nothing seems more important to me than the conversion of the Church, her submitting to herself anew to the rule of God. Humbling ourselves before God will alone suffice to assure that the Spirit can come and take control. Then and then only will sacraments mean something. Then and then only will liturgies come alive. Then and then only will we gain a vision of what God is doing through the new humanity. Then and then only will programs and plans begin to coalesce with the will of God. So long as the churches remain tuned in only to themselves and what they are doing, they will not be effective agents of grace.

Some churches do a remarkable job of midwifery. The Church of the Saviour in Washington, D.C., is an example. There is no crystal cathedral where God is feted under glass,

Sunday by Sunday. Rather, the Church of the Saviour is seven congregations, the result of a self-destruct plan devised by the pastor, Gordon Cosby. It is a coffee house and bookstore that exudes warmth and wisdom for passersby. It is six members of the hard-core unemployed operating a bakery. It is a former convict running a parking lot. It is an apartment corporation composed of members of the Church of the Saviour. It is dozens of groups "calling out the called" to peacemaking, petitioning for economic justice, praying, and other tasks. It is Christ incarnate in metropolis in the lives and actions of people.

Is the Church's task not, first of all, to embody love and grace? Such seems to me to be the point of Colossians 3:12–17. The fruit of the Spirit is not something we strive for; rather, it is something we "put on" and allow to "rule in our hearts" and "dwell in us richly" "in the name of the Lord Jesus." Often it's a struggle to get out of the way and let the Spirit work.

INDIVIDUAL EXPERIENCE

In some contrast to my Baptist forebears, then, I acknowledge the very great importance of considering the corporate channel through which the Spirit works to effect the will of God. At this point, however, I want to examine more carefully the side of the issue in which my forebears had a keen interest, namely, the operation of grace through the individual channel. Over against an excessive emphasis on spontaneous approaches, still emphatically sustained by Frederick Heiler in his classic on *Prayer*, I would suggest that we can enrich our impoverished Southern Baptist tradition by drawing insights from the vast contemplative tradition of Christian history. Above all, the art of contemplation itself should be recovered.

In Protestantism we have been accustomed to thinking about prayer as telling or informing God. That is an element, to be sure. But if we examine Scriptures and the writings of great women and men of prayer, we will find that prayer is, more than anything, communication, conversation, or communion between ourselves as personal beings and God as the Ultimate Personal Reality in the universe. And if they are right, there is another side to prayer—namely, contemplation or listening, not with the outward ear, but with an inner one, "the ear of the heart." Now listening is precisely the aspect of prayer that we have neglected most, and as a consequence, God has difficulty breaking through to "recycle our understanding" (Rom. 12:2; my paraphrase).

How do we listen to God? How do we tune in and turn on to his working in our lives? Scriptures and great teachers of prayer have perceived several ways. One is through nature. You know Psalm 19:

> The heavens are telling the glory of God;
>   and the firmament proclaims his handiwork.
> Day to day pours forth speech,
>   and night to night declares knowledge.

The psalmist recognized, as you and I would, that this is not a matter of physical perception.

> There is no speech, nor are there words;
>   their voice is not heard;
> yet their voice goes out through all the earth,
>   and their words to the end of the world.

Jesus, similarly, cited nature as a parable of divine providence. The birds of the air, so numerous and seemingly so worthless; the lilies of the field, here today and gone tomorrow; even the hairs of our heads, in and out faster than we can count—all remind us of God's paternal and intimate care.

Yet you and I know what difficulties our culture poses for our perceiving of God's message beamed through nature. The problem might be summed up with the word *urbanization*. Urbanization has to do not merely with congestion of population in limited geographical areas but with a way of life. It is a way that, for one thing, removes us from nature. We see the works of human hands more than those of God's hands. Bricks and mortar, honking cars, rumbling trucks, screeching airplanes—all attest human genius and obscure the work of God. It is a way that also distracts us by its busyness and hurriedness. Intent on getting from one place to another, we do not take time to notice what is in between. Modern transportation, boon that it is in so many ways, has probably done more than anything to diminish our sensitivities to nature. Modern communications, moreover, have conspired with psychology in advertising to drive our conscious perception to a deeper and deeper level.

What all of this means is that, if we really want to hear, we will have to recover a faculty that has been withering and atrophying at a rapid pace. The traffic jams people generate to get into state parks on weekends may say something about the inner compulsion we have to get back to nature. Or perhaps it goes further. Perhaps it is true after all as Augustine observed: Within each of us is a homing instinct. God has made us for God, to praise God, and our hearts are restless until they find rest in God. And underneath the restlessness and turmoil of our technological age and culture we are being driven to listen through nature.

A second way of listening is through history. The Hebrews believed history, all history, was especially the means through which God speaks. Thus Cyrus, the Persian king, can be called "the Lord's anointed." Egypt, Babylonia, Assyria, and the other dominant nations too could reveal God and his purpose for Israel. Yet, though he has spoken and speaks through all history, it is through the covenant people that he has made himself and his purpose known in particular. Like nature, history too is parabolic. Inside it there is a story. And if we listen like little children, we will get the message, and the story will mold and shape our lives.

Edward Everett Hale's *Great Stone Face,* an aged classic, illustrates the method. A young lad saw in a natural outcropping of rock on the face of a cliff a great stone face. In it he discerned lines indicating wisdom, courage, and strength. All his life, he meditated on that face. He kept asking, "Who *is* that face?" At the end of his life it dawned on him. That was *he.* He had become what he had discerned there.

The Jewish codified oral tradition of Jesus' day, known as the *Mishnah,* confirms this point in its directions for Passover, or *Pesach.* For observance of the home *seder,* the family Passover meal, the rules direct the youngest person present to ask, "Why is this night different from all other nights?" In response, the head of the family is to tell the story of the Exodus. Here the *Mishnah* adds these instructive words "Do this as if you yourselves were going out in the Exodus from Egypt."

For the Jewish people the Exodus has been the paradigmatic story that stood out above all others. Better than any other, it tells them who they are as the covenant people and how God relates to them as his people. For Christians another story has been the paradigm, the story of the life, death, and resurrection of Jesus of Nazareth. It is not surprising, therefore, that the gospel story has been the focus of Christian meditation par excellence.

Here, too, however, we encounter a difficulty. This problem may be pinpointed by reminding you that, in Western society, we are the heirs of two ways of knowing. I will describe the dominant one first. This is the Greek way of knowing, the way of empirical observation and rational reflection. The Greeks observed with their eyes, listened with their ears, tasted, touched, smelled, and then reflected rationally upon what they gathered by external sensory perception.

The near-complete dominance of Western thinking by the Greek mode of knowing is reinforced by the Puritan approach to Scriptures. Battling Anglicans and Roman Catholics, our Puritan forefathers would allow the use of imagination only on heaven or hell. Scriptures, they contended, must be interpreted rationally and as nearly literally as possible. With this thinking they produced two kinds of heirs. One is Unitarian rationalists, who say that since Scriptures cannot stand up to the canons of modern science, they cannot be given any more credence than any other fanciful set of writings. The other is fundamentalist rationalists, who begin with the assumption that the Scriptures are inerrant and proceed to reject any discoveries of modern science, such as evolution, that will not square with Scriptures. Behind both of these approaches lies an assumption that *truth equals fact*, and fact equals truth. If anything is not factual, it is not true. Thence a strict Fundamentalist will insist on Jesus' parables being literal histories. If Jesus made up a story, he lied. Similarly, Adam and Eve, Jonah, and other biblical accounts must be factual; their truth depends on that.

I am not suggesting that historical-critical studies have no value for understanding the Bible. They have a great deal. What I am trying to say is this: If the message of God through Scriptures is going to mold and shape our lives, we will have to approach the Scriptures also by the other way of knowing, the Hebrew mode, just as the saints of the Middle Ages or Ignatius Loyola did. In the Hebrew view nature is parabolic, history is parabolic, our lives are parabolic. Within them is a story. We must come as little children and enter into the story in imagination. You know how children make a story their own. They blurt out something. They act out part of the story. They interrupt the storyteller. So must we do—going through the life, death, and resurrection of Jesus as our story. God has beamed his message of grace through it.

A third way of listening is through other people. In his classic *On Listening to Another,* Douglas Steere has listed four qualities of a good listener:

The first is vulnerability. Vulnerability comes from the Latin word *vulnus,* meaning wound. A good listener must expose him- or herself, be capable of being hurt. A good listener must know the human situation, like Jesus, "tempted in all points like as we are" (Heb. 4:15).

The second is acceptance. Acceptance belongs to the very essence of *agape.* We take the other at face value. That person does not have to fit our mold before we are willing to hear.

The third is expectancy. Expectancy has to do with hope. Pessimism can intrude. Despair. Yet hopefulness is at the heart of the Christian experience. We uplift the other. Douglas Steere himself has a gift for uplifting others. It would be difficult to describe what that gift is. But I have never gone away from a conversation with him, that I did not feel uplifted by a sense of divine presence.

The fourth is constancy. We might say patience, but constancy is more descriptive. The Latin means "staying with" or "standing with." Most of us will tend to be dragged down in a personal conversation in which another person has difficulty expressing what he or she wants to say. We will begin to say, "Oh, you mean . . ." Of course, we know they don't *mean* that. What we are saying is, "It's time to finish this conversation. Here is something you can say to do so."

Listening means more than hearing. We want to go beyond words and thoughts, to "feel where words come from." We speak often today of nonverbal communication. A tear trickling down a cheek may say more than all the words that have passed between two persons. Many know, too, about a communion of love, love flowing out toward another, binding heart to heart and mind to mind.

Within every conversation, Steere reminds us, there is more than the speaker and the hearer. There is also the person trying so desperately to communicate and the listener. Beyond even these, however, is the Divine Listener, the Divine Spectator. And if we are really listening, we may become the means through which another person communicates not merely with another human being but with the Other, with God. And it may be, if we are really listening, we will discern a message that God is beaming to us through the other person. Grace may burst in upon us.

Once again, however, we must notice a problem that our culture poses for us. It can be captured in the word *distractedness.* Urban society creates a high level of distractedness. We are full of ourselves and what we are doing. We run pantingly and frantically through a crowded calendar of appointments. Our sensory and nervous systems simply refuse to handle more. A few years ago, a New York University psychology student tried an experiment in Central Park. He stood on his head on a park bench for six hours to see how many people would notice. Only a couple of people gave him so much as a sidelong glance. They see so many bizarre occurrences, one more simply failed to faze them.

Could this also explain why for days thousands of people in Denver did not notice an indigent at a bus stop whose feet froze solid? Or why seventy persons stood on a subway platform and watched a young man, arm in a cast, be crushed by an oncoming train, some even jeering at him? Ashley Montague, noted anthropologist and sociologist, says he does not think we can remain human in cities larger than a few thousand. The reason— we cannot retain our compassion.

Here, too, if we listen, we will have to be determined. Nothing less is required than recovery of our atrophied inward faculty.

Brother Lawrence, a seventeenth-century Carmelite lay brother, has put the issue in the proper way. Our goal is to "practice the presence of God." How do we do that? Not by rigorous disciplines, though these may result from what we do, Brother Lawrence learned, but by falling head over heels in love with God. You know what happens when you fall in love with someone: You can't get the beloved out of your mind. Every thought, every act, every word—he or she is there. Yet falling in love with another person is not as automatic as we sometimes assume. Infatuations may happen at first sight, but not true love. To fall deeply in love, you have to get to know the other person. You have to spend time together. You have to listen as well as speak. So, too, the love of God. So listen!

NOTES

1. John A. T. Robinson, *Honest to God* (Philadelphia: Westminister Press, 1963), p. 90.
2. Ibid., p. 97.
3. Ibid., p. 99.
4. Ibid., p. 101.
5. Douglas Rhymes, *Prayer in the Secular City* (Philadelphia: Westminister Press, 1967), p. 40.
6. *Prayer in the Secular City*, p. 46 f.
7. Douglas Rhymes, *Through Prayer to Reality* (Winona, Minn: St. Mary's College Press, 1974), p. 23.
8. Ibid., p. 35.
9. For a fuller critique of Kelsey, see E. Glenn Hinson, "Morton F. Kelsey: Theologian of Experience," *Perspectives in Religious Studies* (Spring 1982), pp. 1–15.
10. George Gallup, Jr., and David Poling, *The Search for America's Faith* (Nashville: Abingdon Press, 1980), pp. 25, 33.
11. Robert Wuthnow, *Experimentation in American Religion: The New Mysticisms and Their Implications for the Churches* (Berkeley, Los Angeles, London: University of California Press, 1978), pp. 144 f.
12. Ibid., pp. 15–43.
13. On survival prospects see Kenneth A. Briggs, "Future of New Religious Movements," in *Religions in America*, ed. Herbert L. Marx, Jr. (New York: H. W. Wilson, 1977), pp. 187–190.
14. Harvey Cox, *Turning East* (New York: Simon & Schuster, 1977), p. 18.
15. Quoted by David Steindl-Rast, "Recollections of Thomas Merton's Last Days in the West," *Monastic Studies* reprint, p. 10.
16. "Christian Obedience" in *Concilium*, ed. Christian Duquoc and Casiano Floristan (New York: Seabury Press, 1981).
17. Tilden H. Edwards, *Spiritual Friend* (New York and Ramsey, N.J.: Paulist Press, 1980), p. 106.
18. Richard J. Foster, *Celebration of Discipline: The Path to Spiritual Growth* (San Francisco: Harper & Row, 1978).
19. Meister Eckhart, "The Eternal Birth," Sermon: IV in *Meister Eckhart*, ed. Franz Pfeiffer, trans. C. de B. Evans (London: John M. Watkins, 1924), p. 25.

V. FAMILY AND PERSONAL RESOURCES

10. Sacred Shelters: Families and Spiritual Empowerment

DOLORES LECKEY

Several assumptions underlie this chapter. One is that Saint Paul was right when, long ago in Athens, he argued that God is not far from each of us, for, "in him we live and move and have our being" (Acts 17:28).

Most of us come to this knowledge that we exist *in God*, not through any esoteric means, but through the ordinary events of family or community living, in the intimacy of *presence* to one another. Obviously, life together does not, *ipso facto*, assure transcendent consciousness. Intentional and attentive reflection in our common life is needed. "To have lived is not enough," says Samuel Beckett in *Waiting for Godot.* "We have to talk about it."

The classic spiritual disciplines can help us "to talk about it." The disciplines include prayer and worship, spiritual direction, confession, the works of mercy, Scripture study—all of these can and do soften the heart so that we may welcome and attend to the stirrings of God within ourselves and within the matrix of our familial relationships.

A second assumption is that authentic Christian spirituality, rooted as it is in the doctrine of the Incarnation, is an inclusive spirituality, one that addresses all aspects of the human person: body and intellect, emotion and spirit, solitude and society.

The third assumption is that the family settings that reveal the fullness of our graced humanity are unique and varied. We grow in the knowledge of God in one-parent as well as two-parent families, in families that live with sickness and brokenness and uncertainty as well as those that enjoy the gifts of health, security, and compatibility. The God of Christianity comes to men and women, not only in the light, but in the darkness as well. Why do I say this? Because of Jesus. Because in my groping to know who God is, who I am, what the meaning of the world is and my relationship to the world, I am reminded of the New Testament affirmation that I can make some sense of these questions by studying the man Jesus (Philippians 2, John 14, and elsewhere).[1]

So it is Jesus of Nazareth in all his human aspects,[2] including his human family, whom I have placed at the center of this chapter, which is a reflection on the family as a sacred shelter. By sacred shelter I mean a place of acceptance, nurture, and growth that empowers family members to participate, according to their unique vocations, in God's ongoing acts of compassion and salvation. The family as a sacred shelter does not draw energy inward in a narcissistic way, nor does it isolate family members from the larger concerns of the society. On the contrary, it releases its members for the pastoral care of the world.

Focusing first on several aspects of the Gospel with respect to Jesus and his particular and unique family, I will touch on the family dynamics embedded in those Gospel stories, particularly those of parenting, and indicate how appropriate those parenting dynamics can be as spiritual resources for social compassion.

I will also identify a few major family issues that have the potential to strengthen the human family to face our uncertain future, not only with compassion, but with inner courage.

ON BEING HUMAN

There are certain obvious difficulties in dealing with the Gospel accounts of Jesus' family. The difficulties arise from the distinction that modern biblical scholarship has created between the truths of faith and those of history. We now know that these accounts of Jesus' family life are informed by postresurrection faith and Christology rather than by factual knowledge of the actual events.[3] This circumstance not withstanding, our evangelical purpose as confessing Christians is, I believe, well served by entering fully into the human and religious truths found in those narratives of Jesus' origins and early family life.

For example, the majestic opening chapter of Matthew that names names in Jesus' human lineage introduces us to Jesus in a highly personal and concrete way. This in itself says something about the importance of our own personal and concrete human histories.

Five women are included in Jesus' genealogy, four of them Old Testament women, and the fifth, "Mary, of whom was begotten Jesus, who is also called the Christ" (Matt. 1:16).

Scripture scholars have analyzed the presence of the four Old Testament women whom Matthew names, and conclude that what they have in common is that they were involved in irregular or extraordinary marital unions. Yet, the scholars point out, through these unions, in which the woman was often the heroic figure, God carried out the divine promises and plans. The women named are Tamar, who got Judah to propagate the messianic line; Rahab, a prostitute whose courage allowed Israel to enter the Promised Land; Ruth, whose initiatives allowed her and Boaz to become great grandparents of King David. The fourth woman mentioned, Bathsheba, intervened with David so that the throne would be passed to Solomon. This devise of Matthew prepares us for the irregular marital situation into which Jesus was born.[4]

And what was that situation like?

Consider the Annunciation, the "Good News" brought to Mary of Nazareth that she is to have a child. Devotionally we have tended to domesticate and flatten this event so much that it is like a Steven Spielberg film: An angel swoops in while Mary is at prayer (at a high Renaissance prie-dieu); Mary is enraptured and the miracle goes forward without a hitch, or at least without a worrisome hitch. Because we've been conditioned to be spectators at the Spielberg film, we know it's going to turn out all right—by our twentieth-century, technological standards.

But remove the total otherness of the Annunciation for a moment and imagine Mary's emotional, mental, spiritual, physical—in short, human—state brought on by this untoward pregnancy.

She was certainly at a decisive crossroad, never an easy place for any human being to be. Luke's account says "she didn't understand." She didn't understand the origins of her pregnancy; she didn't understand how she could go on unmarried, subject to punishment by the law. Indeed, there was a great deal she didn't understand. Yet, in spite of her confusion, we are told she yielded to the life God was creating in her, for her and for us. This yielding of Mary constituted an act of trust in the unsettling ways of God.

And Joseph? The silent and hidden man of the Gospel? What of him? We know little about him, but Matthew does record Joseph's deep disquiet. He had decided to divorce Mary quietly, because she is pregnant and he knows he is not the father. He must have felt betrayed; that is an understandable human emotion. Any man or woman who has experienced betrayal in an intimate love relationship will know something of this man's anguish. I can imagine his exhaustion as he wrestled with his future, until at last he slept—which is what we humans tend to do when life is too much for us. We rest, we wait, we hope for relief. So Joseph slept, and dreamed.

From the deepest part of his slumbering self God's word came to him "Trust Mary. Do not reject her. Be husband to her and father to her child. Be a family." When Joseph awakened, he followed through on his subconscious insight.

Here we have two people who chose to trust the leadings of God and, in so doing, to transcend the conventions of their own society. Jesus was born into a family where it was ordinary to be turned upside down, and where, in the upsidedownness, faith grew strong, so strong that it ultimately conquered death. Jesus was born into a marriage forged out of the most radical kind of trust.

JESUS AT TWELVE

What else do we know about Jesus and his family? Bits and pieces, mostly. One story, however, an account in Luke, is pivotal for understanding the spiritual dynamics of this family. It is the story of Jesus in the Temple.

Now his parents went to Jerusalem every year at the feast of Passover. And when he [Jesus] was twelve years old they went up according to custom. And when the feast was ended, as they were returning, the boy Jesus stayed behind in Jerusalem. His parents did not know it, but supposing him to be in the company, they went a day's journey, and they sought him among their kinsfolk and acquaintances. And when they did not find him, they returned to Jerusalem seeking him. After three days they found him in the Temple, sitting among the teachers, listening to them and asking them questions; and all who heard him were amazed at his understanding and answers. (Luke 2:41–48)

The account goes on: "And when they [that is, Mary and Joseph] saw him they were *astonished;* and his mother said to him, 'Son, why have you treated us so? Your father and I have been looking for you *anxiously.'*"

And what did the twelve-year-old Jesus reply? "How is it that you sought me? Did you not know that I must be in my Father's house?"

His parents' reaction was, it seems to me, again, a very human reaction, that of any parents who experience the first signs of independence and autonomy in their children. According to Luke, "They did not understand the saying which he spoke to them." He went home with them and was obedient, we're told, and his mother "kept all these things in her heart."

Now whether or not this story was appended to Luke's Gospel, along with the infancy narratives, after the public ministry section was written is not immediately relevant to these reflections. What is relevant, I think, is that the story of Jesus at twelve raises important points about families as sacred shelters that allow one to grow strong in the Spirit. These points coalesce around two questions:

The first, and perhaps the overarching question, is *What kind of parenting develops the kind of self-awareness and courage and confidence displayed by Jesus at twelve?*

The second question, more existential and personal, arises from the first one. *Do we really want a child like Jesus at twelve, or twenty, or thirty?*

WHAT KIND OF PARENTING GROWS A CHILD LIKE JESUS AT TWELVE?

Another way to frame the question is to ask what kind of family nurtures prophets and teachers who will minister to the entire human family.

Let's think about families in our own time for a moment. Living as we do in an age of image making, it is not surprising that an ideal family has been constructed for our consumption. And the Church is not exempt from the influence of image making. In the projected ideal there is marital harmony most, if not all, of the time; children are obedient; there is always a well-kept home, regular church attendance, Scouts, good SAT scores, good income, faithful friends, enjoyment of the fruits of the earth.

The trouble with the ideal image is that although it's partially true for many people, it is totally untrue for many more, who see nothing of their own doubt and struggle in the projection of this ideal.

At the other end from the family of the ideal image is the family-in-crisis image of the soap opera. These relationships go from one level of confusion to another. Lust, greed, envy, anger —the list of what we used to call the capital sins predominate. Though this portrayal is probably much closer to real life (which is why half the world watches the soaps), it too is partial. What's missing there is the other side of crisis, namely, redemption, salvation, hope, gratitude.

The kind of family from which Jesus drew life looks to be much closer to the crisis family than to the packaged, idealized version. But—and this is critically important—it was a family that, time after time, trusted God's leadings. From the moment of conception to the moment of crucifixion, Jesus occasioned this movement into ever-deeper levels of trust within his own family.

Modern research confirms what many parents have long known, that children absorb all manner of things from their parental environment, that is, from *who we are*. I expect that Jesus absorbed the attitude of *trusting* the interior movements of the Spirit from the woman and man who nurtured him from the beginning. Out of this *trusting* of his inner experience developed an autonomy and confidence that allowed him to linger in the Temple.

Unfortunately, when we think or talk about Jesus' family, "The Holy Family," there is a tendency to be influenced by "the halo effect." A careful reading of the Scriptures helps us to diffuse the glare of the halo. Mary and Joseph were not benignly indifferent to the independent spirit of their precocious adolescent son. They were not infused with some special knowledge that turned them into play actors. On the contrary, they were troubled and they said so. What they *didn't* do was beat the willfulness out of their Son, either physically, emotionally, or psychologically. They accepted him in all his mystery. And he accepted their authority, aware that it was not an authority for control of him but a vehicle of love. He grew in this environment "in wisdom and stature, and in favor with God and man."[5]

I think both the parents and the child learned something from the Temple event. I think Jesus learned a good bit about parental fidelity. And I think Joseph and Mary learned something every parent must learn: the hard truth that our children are not *ours* in any absolute sense. They are God's children first.

I think a family in which parents and children learn such things from each other can raise up children like Jesus at twelve. This is the kind of parenting I call *empowerment.*

Empowerment is embedded in in the gospel. We see this vividly in the adult ministry of Jesus, especially in the healing episodes, where a pattern of liberation is obvious. First Jesus asked the question, "What do you want?" It was a question that reached deep into the center of personal desire and responsibility, into the will. It was a question full of respect for the other. Jesus, "the embodiment of Good News," did not address others by saying, "This is what *I* want for you," but recognized and affirmed the freedom to choose, which God grants to all people. His question, "What do you want?" called people to believe in their inherent power to be whole. It was (and is) a confronting question; it is also an enabling one. When he was answered truthfully, Jesus tapped the power in the other: "Get up and walk," he said to the paralytic; or *"Your* faith has cured you," to the woman with a hemorrhage, and to the leper, and so on.

If social compassion means this kind of revelation to others— that they are of inestimable value to God, that they are created free and responsible and are asked to participate in the ongoing adventure of creation—then perhaps the first step in nurturing social compassion in our homes is for us, parents, to empower our children as Jesus empowered "the little ones," the Anawim of Israel. This understanding of compassion invites others to celebrate the presence of God already in their lives, even in unlikely places and irregular situations; in strained relationships, in disappointment, in doubt, as well as in love and understanding and accomplishments. In this celebration of valleys and hills is the realization of human freedom. This is the spirit of the Beatitudes.

PARENTS AND EMPOWERMENT

But what does it mean concretely to be an empowering parent in the late twentieth century? I have identified four life positions that I consider essential, not only in my role as parent, but in my day-to-day pilgrimage as a Christian person. I see reflections of these life positions in the story of Jesus at twelve, and certainly in the public ministry—Jesus at thirty.

TRUTHFULNESS

The first life position is that of truthfulness. This includes truthfulness about oneself. By that I mean that we parents must confront our own self-deception and evasions in the clear space that solitude and prayer carve out for us. It means being truthful in our relationships with our children, telling them the truth— our truth. Our children, blessed with an uncanny intuition that is one of the gifts of childhood and adolescence, already know our truth, or a lot of it. It remains for us to articulate it.

Nothing in my recent reading has touched on the depth of value of parental truthfulness more than the memoirs of Eugenia Ginzburg. In *Within the Whirlwind*, the second volume of these memoirs, she tells the reason for writing the details of her many years of political imprisonment under Stalin. It was simply that the truth be known. Her son, who was only four when she was imprisoned, was directly responsible for her undertaking this enormous writing task. When he was sixteen they were reunited for the first time in twelve years. Their first night together they stayed up until dawn talking, reciting poems, connecting with each other at the level of heart and spirit. As the sun appeared in the sky, her son asked her what her life apart from him had been like. She decided to tell him only the truth (she said it could not be the whole truth because no one knew the whole truth, but she would not hide anything from him). That decision was the beginning of her memoirs.

The publication of the first volume, *Journey into the Whirlwind,* brought accolades from her compatriots, artists and writers from Russia and elsewhere. She interpreted this overwhelming reception of her work this way: "It was perfectly clear to me that I owed this not to any special literary merit in the book but solely to its truthfulness. People who had been starved for the simple, unsophisticated truth were grateful to anyone who would take the trouble of telling them, *de profundis,* how it really was." Ginzburg's truth encompassed not only her own experience but also a realistic appraisal of the conditions of the world that she inhabited.

Speaking the truth to and with children ought to include, I believe, some kind of realism. What will it mean to be a Christian in a society that is undergoing unprecedented social and cultural change? Change that includes everything from (*a*) the aging factor (people are living and working longer) to (*b*) a defense posture predicated on stockpiling nuclear weapons to (*c*) an economy that is nonexpansionist and likely to remain so to (*d*) a dramatic shift in social morality, that is, approval of social behaviors society historically disapproved of in this country?

Daniel Yankelovitch and others who have surveyed and written about these changes believe that most adaptation to these changes has been by individuals and voluntary agencies like the churches. But if we are going to survive *as a society* the body politic will also have to adapt. Therefore, to be a Christian in our society—today and tomorrow—must include a sense of mission to the world. Perhaps families need to be about the work of developing appreciation for the lay vocation, the calling to be a parent, to be a politician, to be a researcher, to be a farmer, to be a teacher, to be a Christian layperson fully engaged with the world, respectful of secular work, in the world *awesomely,* a transcendent presence.

Truthfulness in families also means hearing the truth that our children will teach us if we let them. Not only do our children mirror us, our values and our faults, they penetrate the facade of our illusions. They push us "not to fake it." When Mary and

Joseph found the twelve-year-old Jesus in the Temple, he didn't tell them what they wanted to hear. He spoke his truth to them.

TRUST

The second life position for empowerment is trust. Parenthood is certainly one of the great opportunities for learning to let go of the impulses to *control, subdue, possess.* These are the impulses of corrupted power, not freeing power, but they are so dominant in most of us that without an experience like parenthood we can go through life thinking we are in control of everything and putting all our energy into keeping control. The thin line between intervention in another's life and respect for the other's autonomy is the line that parents have to walk during every stage of their children's development. Walking this line we learn over and over again that our children are not ours in any ultimate sense; they are God's, created in the divine image, not our image (although they will be *like* us whether or not we want them to be). Being God's children, they enjoy the gift of freedom and are open to unique experiences of grace.

T. S. Eliot's "Ash Wednesday" prayer to Mary is appropriate for parents struggling with this life position. The poet says to her,

> Teach us to care and not to care
> Teach us to sit still.

This walking of a thin line that is parental trust requires alertness, perceptiveness, concentration, and communication so that we may experience what Christopher Lash calls "the divine virtue of letting be." We might well pray "Ash Wednesday" every day.

RESPECT FOR DIFFERENCES

The third life position of an empowering parent is that of respect for differentiation and differences. This is not to deny the importance of the collective spirit and action that characterize genuine family life. Differentiation and "being different" is not the same as hard individualism and privatism. It is, rather, the realization that God and grace are not reserved for conformity.

As Jesus grew in age and grace, he obviously grew away from his family. The scriptural evidence is that *his* call to evangelize was so powerfully present that his family ties became relatively less important.

Several Gospel accounts record Jesus' differentiation and movement away from family norms and expectations as his ministry gained in intensity. Mark's account is the starkest. There we read that Jesus' family set out to seize him, convinced "he was out of his mind" (Mark 3:21). They wanted to bring him back home, back to his senses, to normality—and they were rebuffed. Jesus declared his family to be those who hear the word of God and keep it. Jesus' natural family seems to be replaced by an eschatological family-community. How do we Christian parents feel about similar movements from family to community?

The story of Enten Eller is a contemporary illustration of parental respect for differentiation. Enter Eller is a student at Bridgewater College in Virginia. He is also a member of the Church of the Brethren. Indicted for failing to register for the draft, he gave his reasons in direct terms. "I have not registered in order to be faithful to God, my conscience, and my church."

At the time of his indictment he faced up to five years in prison and a ten-thousand-dollar fine. As a member of one of three historic peace churches, he would not have had any trouble securing conscientious objector status, but for this young man the probability of CO status was not enough. He could not reconcile himself to cooperating with the Selective Service. People who know him were quick to note that he is not a religious fanatic and not a judge of those who do register for the draft. In fact Enten Eller himself said that many registrants he knows are committed Christians, just as committed as he is. "God calls us to different places," is his response. Not everyone in the Church of the Brethren agreed with Enten's reasons. Among those with a different point of view were his parents. His father, himself a CO during World War II, said, "I personally could register; I would not be happy about it but I could. I do have great respect for his courage in following his own conviction. We [his mother and I] fully support Enten, even though it's not what we would do" (reported in the *Washington Post,* July 12, 1982).

In August of 1982 Enten Eller was convicted of refusal to

register for the draft and was sentenced to 250 hours of community service. He was also ordered by the court to register, which he refused to do. He was then resentenced for violation of his parole, this time to two years of alternate service in a Veterans Administration hospital. He will begin this alternate service in June of 1983, after his graduation from college.

Throughout all of this judicial maze, Enten Ellen made it clear that his life is to follow God wherever that takes him. "That's what I've got to work with," he said.

Echoes of Jesus at twelve?

ACTIVE COMPASSION

The fourth life position that I believe is important if parents are to empower their children is that of active compassion. By that I mean efforts to live the faith of the gospel, in families, by paying attention to those who dwell with us. This kind of attentiveness leads to the recognition of others' needs as well as others' gifts. It is a position that values doing the gospel more than feeling it.

Most parents realize that their children have different needs. The difficulty sometimes is how to correctly identify the need and how to respond to it with generosity. Sometimes we can fail to see the need in a child or young person who is not very demanding.

One of my sons, now twenty-one, is an intensely private person, not given to displays of feeling or long discourses about what he thinks is important. He's always been that way, and being in the middle of four children born close together, it has been easy for me to forget that perhaps he has something on his mind.

The summer when he was twenty there seemed to be a particular kind of tension between us. One day when I was going through *my* list of things I wanted him to do, he looked at me in a strange way. I said, "Tommy, am I nagging you?" He answered, "That's the only time you ever talk to me any more—when you're nagging me about something."

We didn't say any more to each other then. A few evenings later, just before dinner, I asked him to look at my new bookcase and see if he could use that kind in his room. He immediately went to inspect it and was gone for quite a while.

He came back to the kitchen carrying Ernest Becker's *Denial of Death.* "Have you read this, Mom?" "Yes," I said, "last Good Friday."

He opened to the chapter on Kierkegaard. "I wrote a paper on this chapter for one of my courses," he said. "Would you like to read it?" I told him I would.

He went off to get if while I secretly wondered if he could find anything in the chaos called his room—the subject of much of my nagging!

He was back in a few minutes with the paper . . . which I read . . . and reread, and I wondered how I would begin to talk with him about it without sounding like a teacher.

A week or so went by during which I had the opportunity to see my spiritual director. With this new piece of data he began to highlight for me what was going on. My son, now a young man, wants a real relationship with me, he pointed out. He doesn't want to talk about his room; he wants to talk about ideas and feelings, and himself. He wants to know my ideas and feelings— me, as a person. My spiritual director, who knows me well, suggested I might need to be more concentrated on Tommy to see his need at a particular moment.

I decided to pick up the Kierkegaard conversation on the phone. I called Tommy at his summer job. "I take it you are suspicious of mixing up psychoanalysis and religious experience." "That's right," he said. I told him that I didn't make such a severe distinction but that I surely needed to read his tightly packed paper again.

The telephone conversation continued that night "face to face" after dinner. Tommy told me that Becker's motivation for writing the book was his own imminent death. The dishes lay on the table; I wanted another glass of water; there were books waiting to be read and letters to be written—all my compulsions toward functionalism—but, by the grace of God, I realized that those fifteen minutes were shaping the contours of our relationship. I stayed and we talked. And it was good.

What I sense I must do—or continue to do—with my son, is to become active in this way over and over again, to strengthen our burgeoning adult relationship. I must guard against "fading away," as the hero of Walker Percy's *Second Coming* frequently did. I do not want the passion within my son to fade for want of my caring. I want it to burn as vigorously as possible, so that he never doubts he lives. I want it to warm the lives of the people he touches now and will touch in the future.

I have spoken about this intimate episode from my own family life only because I think it is not uncommon for parents to linger in the guardianship role that we wear so comfortably. We are used to taking care of our children. But the day comes when children touch their own power, and it falls to us to let it be so. Bernard Lonergan's transcendental imperatives, "be attentive, be intelligent, be reasonable, be responsible, develop, and, if necessary, change" are remarkably applicable to active compassion in parenthood. The challenge to our imaginations is to re-define and re-establish a relationship of co-responsibility.

These four life positions—truthfulness, trust, respect for differentiation and difference, and active compassion—are not so separate and discrete as this chapter implies. Rather, they weave in and out of each other as a process for empowering our children.

DO WE REALLY WANT A CHILD LIKE JESUS?

The second question that the story of Jesus at twelve raises is Do we *really* want a child like that? A nonconformist? One who challenges our own belief system and way of life?

The child psychiatrist and writer Robert Cole's book *The Privileged Ones* is about children who come from very comfortable backgrounds. One of the stories is about a child whose religious questioning was so disturbing to his parents that he was sent to see a psychiatrist. In an interview in *Sojourners,* Coles, who has written previously about very poor and destitute children, said, "This is the most devastating story I've ever written."

It is the story of a child who grew up in a very rich Florida family, and whose experience in the Presbyterian church somehow got to him when he was nine, ten, or eleven and prompted him to be very scrupulously concerned with the teachings of Christ. It got to the point that he was talking about them in school, upsetting teachers and fellow students by repeating certain statements that Christ made—namely, that it would be awfully hard for rich people to get into heaven (even though the child himself was very rich), that the poor would indeed inherit the moral and spiritual kingdom, and so forth.

The more he talked like this, the more of a "problem" he became for his teachers, his parents, and eventually for a local pediatrician. Ultimately this boy ended up in psychotherapy, because it was felt that he had what was "a problem" and needed help. His parents were told to stop taking him to church.

And, Coles was asked, did they "help" him? Coles: "Well, they did 'help' him and he lost a lot of these Christian preoccupations and became another American entrepreneur."[6]

I think to some extent we all want our children to live up to the expectations we have for them, and if they hear a different drummer, the tendency often is to interpret that as rebellion or rejection. The Florida story in the Coles book is not a new story. We've heard it before, often in the lives of the saints. But the Florida boy's story has a different ending from, say, that of Catherine of Siena, Thomas Aquinas, or Saint Francis of Assisi—all of whom chose a different path from the one their parents decided for them.

Catherine Benincasas, known to history as Catherine of Siena, is described by her biographers as a "take-charge person." She was a strong-willed child, and throughout her girlhood she evidenced a pattern of behavior that could accurately be called parental defiance. A decisive inner experience impelled her to follow her own way, which she identified as God's will for her. For a long time this put her at odds with her family. Only gradually did her family recognize and support her mission, namely, the religious and political reformation of the Italian states.

If Catherine of Siena were transported across time and space to now, no doubt she and her network of relatives would be in family therapy, which *sometimes* serves as the acceptable equivalent of beating the willfulness out of a child. (I hasten to add that there are psychiatrists who agree with this assessment.)

The point is that to be the parent of a child like Catherine, or the boy in Florida, or Enten Eller, or Jesus, is not necessarily fun. Parenting a prophetic child draws the parent into the spiral of change—conversion and transformation—which most of us resist in one way or the other because it hurts. One is required to give up so much. We must give up having a closed mind and spirit; we must give up the false security of possessing other people (or thinking we possess them). We, and our children, too, must give up the absolute claims of family on our energy and life direction. What we gain, though, is courage and willingness to engage with the world so loved by God.

TOWARD THE FUTURE

All families in these last days of the twentieth century live in the shadow of the unspeakable. To some extent we are numbed by feelings of impotence. The world requires so much ministering, and one family is so little in the face of so much need. How can we get in touch with the lifesprings of our own power, and how can we free that power for the sake of the world?

Ancient spiritual wisdom teaches that maturity and compassion begin when we cease running away from our lives. The dicta take many forms: "Dig your own well." "Bloom where you are planted." "The Kingdom of God is in your midst."

This does not mean that the well digging or the flower cultivation or the looking within is easy. It is just true. Attention and appreciation of the learnings implicit in the ordinary activities of family life can invest the whole enterprise with fresh meaning. Family life has a certain relentlessness to it, and that's good. It shapes the virtues of perseverance and fortitude; it wears away the sharp edges of self-assertion and ego-importance. By the same token, growth in intimacy, whether between spouses or parents and children, or among siblings, affirms our true worth, that is, our unique being in God. Love breeds inner freedom, and neither bombs nor concentration camps nor an unjust economic policy can kill that free being.

At the heart of family life is what is popularly called nurturing, that is, the making of a home, the education of the young, the evoking of the giftedness in adult members. Traditionally women have been the nurturers, the ones doing domestic pastoral care. Now, and in the future, the collaborative and caring skills developed by women as a group are being sought in the public arenas of society.[7]

In the Apostolic Exhortation on "The Role of the Christian Family," Pope John Paul II urged that attention be given to the promotion of women's several roles, that is, to the harmonious combination of family roles with public, professional roles (Article 23). At the same time the Pope asked that domestic and nurturing roles not be devalued. Rather, a theology of work needs to be developed, he said, to promote greater understanding of what comprises *true* work, including educating society to the awareness that the work of women in the home is as much authentic work as business or law or medicine, or anything else (Article 23).

The papal exhortation comes at a time when men are learning to share more fully and directly in the domestic responsibility of home and child care. In many instances this has been occasioned by women's insistence on the justice of sharing domestic responsibility, particularly when they, too, are employed outside the home. But it is also a matter of a new consciousness on the part of men about the meaning of parenthood. Fathers who are with their wives through the birth experience tell of the intense bonding they experience with their children. They want to be intimately engaged in the day-to-day infant care that is so formative for both child and parent. The fruits of this parental sharing may extend beyond the walls of the nursery.

Studies of survivors of World War II concentration camps reveal that women prisoners were not so likely to lose the sense of life's meaning as were men. This has been interpreted in terms of men's reliance on external validation of the self: career, success, money, community respect. Women, on the other hand, were accustomed to internal validation: meeting their responsibilities for feeding the children, tending to relationships, developing inner vision. It seems reasonable to me to assume that as more and more men actively participate in the nurturing dynamics of home life they, too, will increasingly turn inward for meaning and self-valuing. This can prove to be a spiritual treasure in times of crisis.

Beyond the social value of nurturing in families there lies a unique, organic reality, a genetic unity that does not exist in any other social unit. Eugenia Ginzburg encountered the full force of this reality when she was reunited with her sixteen-year-old son.

A friend, Julia, accompanied Eugenia Ginzburg to the flat

where her son was waiting in the company of Communist officials. One of the officials, a woman, thought it would be amusing if the boy were not told which woman was his mother. She ushered both women into the room and told the boy he must choose. Ginzburg writes:

He did not hesitate between Julia and myself. He came up to me and self-consciously put his hand on my shoulder. And then I heard at long last the word that I had been afraid of never hearing again, that now came to me across a gulf of almost twelve years, from the time before all courts, prisons, and penal drafts, before the death of my first-born, before all those nights in Elgen.

"Mother," said my son, Vasya. . . . and then in a rapid whisper into my ear, "Don't cry in front of them. . . . "

Thereupon I took hold of myself. I looked at him in the way that those who are really close, who know everything about one another, who are members of the same family, look at one another. He understood my look. It was the most crucial moment in my life: the joining up of the broken links in our chain of time; the recapturing of our organic closeness severed by twelve years of separation, of living among strangers. My son! And he knew, even though I hadn't said a word to him, who *we* were and who *they* were. He appealed to me not to demean myself in their presence.

At last, Ginzburg took her son to their one-room home. There they had their first talk (mentioned earlier in this chapter). About this night of learning about each other she writes:

We were delighted that each of us recognized himself in the other. How astonishing, how really astounding are the laws of genetics. Magical! This child, who remembered neither his father nor his mother, resembled both of them not only in appearance but also in his tastes, his prejudices and his habits. . . . Like me, he too found in poetry a bulwark against the inhumanity of the real world.

She goes on:

The glow of our first talk . . . lit up my relations with my son through all the years that were to come. There were many ups and downs. . . . when the difficult moments came I always called to mind the clear, unsullied spring within him which was revealed to me that night. . . . Today my forty-three-year-old son is as much my friend and comforter as that boy who arrived in Magadan with a small volume of Blok in a shabby rucksack.[8]

Within the sacred shelter of home, love can be practiced and refined and appropriated as a way of life. The love will not stay within the walled limits of a particular home or family for, as Thomas Aquinas aptly noted, love is diffusive of itself. It spills out and runs like a river beyond the family to fill all the crevices and openings of human need.

CONCLUSION

I once knew a man who, with his wife, built a house in the Minnesota woods. They gave life to their children there, and taught them many things: psalms and poems and stories of great men and women. They taught their children respect for the intellectual life, the spiritual life, and the life of manual labor. The man is dead now, and his grown children abide all over the earth. They are lawyers and writers, carpenters and artists, politicians, business persons, and parents. They are caring citizens in a variety of communities.

One daughter wrote a poem about her father at the time of his death. It captures for me the inner life of a family, the ever-present resources for social compassion.

> It will not do to heap his grave with flowers,
> Flowers wilt and die.
> Rather let us shelter as he has sheltered.
> Gather words soft-spoken, deliberate love-tipped,
> Deep-rooted thoughts, nursed with tolerance,
> More vital even than the cinder-block and wood,
> These walls he built have made the world home for us.
> And this great gift remains good:
> Because he was, we are ourselves.
> And the flowers cannot do for him.
> He is living still:
> So still, there is no longer breath.
> So living he is beyond all death.[9]

NOTES

1. Edward Schillebeeckx, O.P., in a lecture delivered at the Trinity Institute, New York City, on January 26, 1983, emphasized that Jesus' life is summed

up in his love of humankind, saying that "Jesus is a human being like you, like me . . . except he is *more* human and more *humane.*"

2. The Third General Council of Constantinople declared unequivocally that Jesus of Nazareth, the Crucified One, he whom his followers called the Christ, was truly human.

3. See Raymond Brown's *The Birth of the Messiah: Commentary on the Infancy Narratives in Matthew and Luke* (New York: Doubleday, 1977).

4. *Mary in the New Testament,* ed. Raymond E. Brown, Karl P. Danfried, Joseph A. Fitzmeyer, and John Neumann (Philadelphia: Fortress Press; and New York: Paulist Press, 1978).

5. I am indebted to Dr. Robert Hughes, Episcopal priest and theologian, currently on the faculty of the Seminary of the University of the South, for his insights into the parental meaning of the story of Jesus at twelve in the Temple.

6. *Sojourners,* April 1982.

7. Cf. Dr. Jim Baker Miller's *Toward a New Psychology of Women.*

8. Eugenia Ginzburg, *Within the Whirlwind,* trans. Ian Boland (New York: Harcourt Brace Jovanovich, 1981), pp. 264–267.

9. This poem was written by Mary Hynes Berry on the occasion of her father's death. It is published here with permission.

11. Love, Violence, and Apocalypse

GERALD G. MAY

It was on Martin Luther King's birthday in 1983 that I first sat down to consider what I could write about spiritual resources in a time of apocalypse. Also, Richard Attenborough's film *Gandhi* was just opening in neighborhood theaters. As spiritual revolutionaries, both King and Gandhi searched for truly peaceful ways of resisting violence, ways that would not stir up further violence within oneself or others. It seems that now, of all times, it is vital to continue this search. The greatest irony and saddest fact of revolution has always been that in trying to overcome violence and oppression, one tends to breed more of it. The peace demonstrations of the sixties are a good example of this. As passive as many of the demonstrators were, their acts of resistance often created so much anger in the authorities and in the "establishment" that overall violence increased rather than decreased. I think true pacifists like King and Gandhi would understand that this occurred because, regardless of the peacefulness of the demonstrators' external behavior, many of them harbored anger and contempt in their hearts rather than love.

We may hope that American society learned a lesson from that experience. It may be an unconscious lesson; we may not understand the spiritual and psychological reasons why passive resistance can contribute to violence, but many of us are left with a clear sense that some kind of radically different approach is needed. In my opinion, this fresh approach must be rooted in a concern for how we, as peacemakers and nonviolent resisters of death and oppression, actually *feel* toward the people we are called to resist.

For me, the most important teaching of Martin Luther King

and Mohandas Gandhi is also one of the teachings of Jesus Christ; in any encounter with evil, we must have love in our hearts and we must absolutely trust in the goodness of God and God's call. We are enjoined by Christ not only to love God and our neighbors but also to love our enemies. This seems a hard enough task by itself, and it has led a number of people to believe that Christians should be nonresistant or even compliant with injustice in the cause of "turning the other cheek." But if we are to try to follow Jesus' example as well as his words, it is impossible to remain uninvolved. Jesus stood up to Satan, threw money changers out of the Temple, and stepped in to stop the unjust stoning of a woman.

Somehow, then, we are asked not only to love our enemies but to resist them *while* we are loving them. I would propose that a partial answer to this challenge lies in a radical, absolute, and wordlessly *contemplative* trust. It is, I think, something reflected in 1 Peter 1:13. "Free your minds, then, of encumbrances: control them, and put your trust in nothing but the grace that will be given you when Jesus Christ is revealed." It is only in such absolute trust that love can be fully energized for nondestructive action.

PASSIVE AND ACTIVE AGGRESSION

If there is no real love in our hearts for those we resist, our resistance will always contain aggression. At best, it will be *passive aggression*. Passive aggression is probably better for the world than active aggression, but simply because it is aggression, it cannot really further the cause of true love.

Early in my psychiatric residency, I encountered the following example of passive and active aggression: Two young servicemen got in trouble with their sergeant when he told them to rake up some leaves. The first man, full of frustrated fury at continually having to take orders, told the sergeant, "Go to hell." When the sergeant tried to put him on report, the man attacked him and wound up in the stockade. This was, of course, active aggression. The second young man, full of the same kind of frustration but having a more even-tempered personality (or perhaps fancying himself a nonviolent resister), proceeded to rake the leaves, but only one leaf at a time. Seeing this, the sergeant yelled at him, "Get a move on, or you'll do the whole area by yourself!" So the young man speeded up his raking, but still only one leaf at a time. This was passive aggression, and it made the sergeant even angrier than he had been with the first man. His orders were being followed to the letter, but the job wasn't getting done and he felt stymied. Finally, when a third man came up to ask the sergeant a question, the sergeant exploded. A major altercation followed, resulting in a number of men being disciplined, including the sergeant himself.

Which was the better way of resisting? Active aggression involves direct violence and a strong likelihood of physical injury, but it does tend to be finished rather quickly, and it is likely to remain confined to a given situation. Similarly, though passive aggression may avoid outright violence, it spreads tentacles of destructiveness beyond the immediate situation. Thus, regardless of whether resistance takes active or passive forms, it tends to be destructive if it comes from an aggressive, unloving heart.

If there is to be hope for moving into confrontations with evil in a truly constructive way, one's actions must somehow come from love. The important question, then, is how we can discover true love for the people whose destructive or evil behavior must be resisted. This is where contemplative resources become imperative. Personal contemplative experience nurtures an ever-deepening realization that God acts grace-fully and constructively through us when we are not trying to run the world by ourselves. When we recognize our utter dependence upon God, and surrender *to* God, it is finally possible to be in deep and total love with God and all God's children. As I see it, this is the foundation for our becoming, through grace, true instruments of God's peace.

In the absence of contemplative experience, it is still possible to force oneself into *acting as if* one loved one's enemies. Much Christian charity comes from this sort of enterprise. When true love cannot be felt, it is clearly best to try to behave in loving ways. It is even possible that in the simple conduct of loving acts, one may begin to feel some tenderness. Both Christian and non-Christian Scriptures indicate this, and so do research studies of behavioral psychology. If one's mind cannot change one's feelings, sometimes a change in behavior can alter *both* thoughts and feelings. But this is not always the case. Sometimes, forcing loving behaviors on oneself in the absence of truly loving feelings produces repression rather than transformation. Then one winds up feeling depressed, embittered, and victimized. Thus, we cannot put any absolute trust in our personal ability to accomplish truly effective psychological self-manipulations in the name of Christianity.

Our fullest hope, I think, lies in the actual, experiential, very solid discovery of a love pre-existing within ourselves for God and for all our sisters and brothers. This love may be commanded of us by Jesus' words, but it comes to us only as Christ's gift. It is not something that can be achieved solely through autonomous willpower or purity of intent. It is not our personal accomplishment. It exists within us only because God has loved us first. The practical issue, then, is not how to accomplish his love but how to *realize* it, how to find it, see it, and experience it where it already exists within us.

CONTEMPLATION AND COMPASSION

My mind tends to see this situation in concrete images. It is as if the deep, awesome love out of which we are created, and that sustains us daily, is layered over with level upon level of self-importance. This self-importance may appear as defensiveness, fear, envy, pride, worry, desire, attachment, or any number of other normal, fully human thoughts and emotions. Most of the time, this surface material is all we consciously feel. It is only in relatively rare moments that this clutter clears for us, and we can really experience the truth of who we are. In such moments we encounter our *true* self-importance, an importance given to us through the absolute love out of which we have been created. It is an importance that exists completely as gift, in no way connected with personal accomplishment.

These moments of true seeing are contemplative, but they do not always occur in prayer or in other obviously religious contexts. For many people, such moments may be encountered more often in nature, in loving relationships, in crisis, or in some artistic context. All such moments are characterized by a tempo-

rary suspension of self-consciousness and personal self-importance occuring within a wide-awake state of awareness. It has
been my experience that such times occur to everyone, regardless of religious or spiritual orientation. It is such an orientation,
however, that makes an all-important difference in how these
moments are received, interpreted, and integrated. If, for example, one experiences such a time without any spiritual understanding whatsoever, one is very likely to interpret it as a temporary, somewhat pleasurable feeling that is completely isolated
from any larger considerations. A purely psychological interpretation would see such times as momentary alterations of awareness. Although prolonged or especially strong experiences of
this kind may on occasion force one into legitimate spiritual reflection, the more common short-lived experiences are often dis-
regarded and forgotten when there is no spiritual context within
which to interpret them.

If such a context does exist, however, such moments are likely
to be seen as gifted visions into the true nature of oneself and of
reality as a whole. Given the proper context, these are recognized as pure experiences of God's love. Within them, we are
granted a sense of the love out of which we have been created,
the love that sustains us in each moment, and the love that is
always within us as a potential source for action in the world.
When this love is recognized, prayer becomes contemplative, at
once a way of moving toward this love and of calling upon it as a
means of helping oneself and others. Further, it is out of this
deep ground of love that we experience ourselves being called to
act for the benefit of the world.

Within a Christian context, this kind of experience—or even
simply the knowledge that such experience exists—is informed
and illumined by the truth of the risen Christ. It therefore not
only speaks of our true nature but of our salvation and our destiny. Thus, in a way, every time we encounter a truly contemplative moment, we are confronted with our own apocalypse.

This apocalypse-in-microcosm is of the deepest significance
for true Christian action. It is only with the dying of our private
self-importance, however briefly or incompletely, that who we
really are is *revealed, uncovered,* for us. This is, after all, the true
meaning of the word *apocalypse;* a revelation of Truth. Once

one's true nature is perceived in this context, then every action can—at least theoretically—become an action of self-giving compassion. There is no room for violence here, because the attachments and self-centeredness that lead to violence have been washed away in the blood of Christ, in the saving act of God's supreme act of love for us. Action coming from such a base can never cause any ultimate destructiveness. Resistance springing from such a source, however active or passive it may be, is not aggression. Instead, it is the fierce, fiery, face of Love.

What I have been describing here may seem idealistic. To be sure, most of us seem to spend most of our time attached to our personal self-importance and thereby feeling separate and removed from the dynamic depths of God's love. It is out of *this* base that most of our daily action comes, and it is here that we are capable of violence, of active or passive aggression that adds to destructiveness rather than healing. When we are truly caught in such attachment, it is impossible to feel much of God's true love in our hearts. All we can do is try to act in loving ways. As I have said, while this kind of action should not be confused with true compassion or Christian charity, it is not to be disparaged. It is endlessly better than giving in to personal desires for destruction. Often such attempts are the best we can do to live by Christ's teachings in the midst of our attachments and self-importance.

If, however, we forget that we are *trying* to live Christian lives and begin to believe we really *are* accomplishing the example of Christ, we can perhaps become more destructive than ever. This kind of "mistake" has been made many times in history, when people have been killed, families destroyed, souls disparaged, in the name of Christ. If we are honest, I think all of us can identify a number of occasions when we ourselves have made such errors, when we have used our faith as an excuse to be selfish and destructive.

However, we can also identify times when we have indeed acted from true compassion, when we have given of ourselves naturally and spontaneously without any thought of personal gain, when our sense of God's love was abundant enough to call us into compassionate action of such clarity and accuracy that all we could do was stand aside and be grateful for the wondrous mystery of grace. Ironically, we may have a little more trouble remembering these times than those when we were more selfish. There is no cause for pride, no occasion for self-aggrandizement, when true compassion is active. There is only wonder, and perhaps a little fear, and sometimes this makes such moments difficult to remember. Yet I would maintain that such memories do exist for each of us, and it would be well to try to recall some of them.

DISCERNMENT AND PRAYER

I do not suggest this recollection simply as a matter of appreciation of grace. I think it holds, in addition, some hope of being a specific spiritual resource for our action in a time that appears apocalyptic. If you spend some time trying to recall moments of action when you really were free of self-service and in touch with God's love, and if you can recover some sense of your state of mind and feelings at the time, you will have acquired a good measuring stick for the consideration of future action. For example, if you are considering some action against nuclear armament or some demonstration against oppression, how do your feelings about this proposed action compare with the feelings you had at a time of true compassion?

Most actions springing from a heartfelt sense of God's love are associated with a deep sense of peace, of vast freedom, and of inner relaxation. In contrast, actions arising from self-service or personal attachment are more associated with restlessness, restrictiveness, and the kind of tension that feels like "I have to . . . ," "I absolutely must . . . ," or "If I can't have this, I'll die." Many readers will perceive immediately that I am talking about classical discernment issues here; these kinds of considerations have been identified with Christian contemplative spirituality for centuries. But words alone cannot describe the feeling-states involved. That is why it is so helpful to try to recall moments of closeness to God, moments of the presence of divine love in action within one's own personal history.

These considerations can be very helpful in trying to clarify the source of intended action. In fact, most classical discernment methods can be used in this regard. By themselves, however, they comprise only a diagnostic tool; they help us make enlightened guesses about the sources of our motivation. But they still do not tell us how to actually *feel* the absolute love for God and neighbor to which Christ has called us. Here we must leave discernments and diagnoses and open our hearts with the deepest humility to the God who alone can grant us this experience of lovingness as a freely given gift. Here we must surrender our intents and agendas and honestly express the depth and limitations of our willingness to do God's will at any given time. This is prayer itself, an absolutely essential time given in openness and honesty to God. Regardless of the specific form such prayer takes (and it may take many forms), it needs to be honest. It needs to express the hopes and fears, desires and resistances, one truly feels at the time. It does little to pray in the way one thinks one should pray, or to try to be the kind of person one thinks one should be in prayer. But it does much simply to be honest. It is essential to say, "Thy will be done," and it is also essential to honestly express one's fears, doubts, and sense of limitation about the extent to which one is truly willing to let that will be done. Perhaps this is what Peter meant in speaking of "the spiritual honesty which will help you to grow up to salvation—now that you have tasted the goodness of the Lord" (1 Pet. 2:2–3).

In the context of this discussion, prayer is the most important contemplative resource for compassion. It is an enterprise that extends us toward the love we must realize if we are to be true peacemakers, a love we cannot achieve but must receive into our hearts as an absolute gift. Put another way, prayer is an endeavor to receive the immediate, felt realization of Christ's having saved us, free from the clutter of our surface attachments. It is a hoping for the grace to cut through these preoccupations, so we might once again realize the endless reservoir of God's love that always exists just beyond them. Prayer in this way is asking for a gift, the gift of awareness of the very love Christ commanded us to have. It is also an honest expression of the extent to which we are willing to receive this gift and its consequent demands for action.

In addition, prayer itself can be a discernment. What does it mean, for example, if you cannot find the time for quiet, intentional prayer, if you are so busy with your action that there is no space for directly opening yourself to God? Or what does it mean when you do sit down to pray and your mind is constantly filled with the busy-ness of the action of your life? During the rest of the day, how much of your action is rooted in ongoing prayer? Especially in resistance and social action, what is the nature of your moment-by-moment prayer?

SPIRITUAL GUIDANCE

Often there are no ready answers to such questions. Sometimes we interfere with prayer as a way of avoiding the truth. This may happen when we are planning an action that we want to label "spiritual" but that is really self-serving, or when we are afraid of what God might require of us. At other times, our prayer is actively interfered *with* by forces seeking to subvert our true spiritual intent. This may happen when we are at the precipice of a very significant action. And sometimes, as the "masters" of spirituality testify, God removes the sense of God's presence from us for God's own reasons. There is no way we can accurately perceive the differences among these possibilities by ourselves. In such circumstances, we simply must avail ourselves of good spiritual guidance. To be adequate, this guidance must come from four sources; from the *teachings* of one's own tradition, from other *people* in the community of that tradition, from the *Scripture* of that tradition, and finally, from one other person who has access to prayer and with whom one can be fully candid.

If, then, we are honest in our own prayer and seek the guidance of our community and tradition, we can at last relax. We can relax not so much in the knowledge that we have done what we can do but in the trust that God is good, that God cares, and that in Christ and through our own willingness, God is taking care of the world. In the final appraisal of things, I would suggest that such relaxation-in-trust is in itself a real resource for spiritual compassion. It is not the kind of relaxation that prohibits action, but a wide-awake, ready, immediate, and flexible state of body and mind that at once expresses God's peace as well as God's strength.

IN CONCLUSION

These, then, are the spiritual resources that I feel may allow us to resist violence and evil in ways that are healing rather than destructive:

1. The knowledge that aggressive resistance, be it active or passive, will contribute to violence.
2. An admission that we cannot, of our own isolated volition achieve the kind of felt love for our enemies that Christ calls us to.
3. A recognition that when the realization of such love does come, it comes as God's gift to us, through Christ's eternally saving act.
4. The possibility of discerning the legitimacy of intended action through prayerful reflection and recollection of past graced events in our lives.
5. The active and regular use of very honest, very human prayer in both active and quiet forms.
6. The willingness to consult with our tradition, community, Scripture, and with one other person who can be our spiritual guide.
7. Finally, a continual decision to risk relaxing in the trust of God's absolute goodness.

Obviously, there is not much new in these suggestions. Most of this information has been around for millennia. But for as long as this knowledge has been available, human beings have been forgetting it. My hope for myself and for our time is that, through grace and our own intentions, these old ideas and practices may be integrated with and informed by modern understanding, that they might come alive again, full of fresh hope, and that they might thereby enable us to remember who we really are in Christ and what we really can be for the world.

Index